Whiteha Watching

Reflections on innovation, inertia and ineptitude in British government (2003-2008)

Colin Talbot

© ENGAGE Public Policy Ltd 2017

All rights reserved.

ISBN-13: 978-1974306343

ISBN-10: 1974306348

Whitehall Watching

CONTENTS

| Chapter 1. | INTRODUCTION | 6 |

SECTION 1.   WHITEHALL WATCHING   15

Chapter 2.	Walking the walk	18
Chapter 3.	A hard Act to follow	24
Chapter 4.	Bring on the professionals	31
Chapter 5.	Cutting the Treasury down to size	34
Chapter 6.	Back to the future	37
Chapter 7.	If at first you don't succeed	40
Chapter 8.	The more things change	43
Chapter 9.	The thick of it	46
Chapter 10.	Too clever for our own good	51
Chapter 11.	An unholy mess	54

SECTION 2.   STRUCTURAL ADJUSTMENTS   59

Chapter 12.	What's in a name	60
Chapter 13.	The ministry of silly changes	63
Chapter 14.	The more things change	66
Chapter 15.	Red tape and chaos theory	69
Chapter 16.	Big is beautiful (again) – with Carole Johnson	72
Chapter 17.	What goes around comes around	78
Chapter 18.	Whitehall shake-up – a premiership starter for No 10	81

SECTION 3.   PUBLIC SPENDING   84

Chapter 19.	The Growing Crisis in Government (Under) Spending	85
Chapter 20.	It's politics, not planning	91
Chapter 21.	Curiouser and curiouser	97
Chapter 22.	There's no debate	100
Chapter 23.	Open the books?	103
Chapter 24.	Gordon keeps the goal posts moving on public spending	107
Chapter 25.	CSR put on ice for Brown premiership	110

Chapter 26.	Darling's big day offers him little room to manoeuvre 113
Chapter 27.	Beam me up, Scottie 115
SECTION 4.	**PERFORMANCE AND EFFICIENCY 120**
Chapter 28.	A false economy 122
Chapter 29.	Economical with the numbers...............128
Chapter 30.	Measure for measure................................131
Chapter 31.	I don't like Mondays – with Carole Johnson and Jay Wiggan 137
Chapter 32.	Mine's a skinny CPA 143
Chapter 33.	Semi-detached savings............................148
Chapter 34.	The value of everything 151
Chapter 35.	21st century public services – putting (some) people first 156
Chapter 36.	Who's the weakest link now?................158
Chapter 37.	Performance anxiety – with Carole Johnson 165
Chapter 38.	No value in secrecy 171
Chapter 39.	You talkin' to me?......................................174
Chapter 40.	Are we being served?...............................177
Chapter 41.	Skills for government? 180
Chapter 42.	Slimming down the targets 183
Chapter 43.	The efficiency of falling productivity..186
Chapter 44.	Reviewing the situation...........................190
SECTION 5. 196	**GOVERNANCE AND POLITICAL ECONOMY**
Chapter 45.	Fall and rise of the state 197
Chapter 46.	A Rock and a hard place 201
Chapter 47.	Democratic ghost in the machine.........204
Chapter 48.	A delicate constitution 207
FOREIGN AFFAIRS	**212**
Chapter 49.	Tough on Terrorism, Tough on the Causes of Terrorism 213
Chapter 50.	JAPAN – Whole lot of shaking up going on 217

Chapter 51.	FRANCE – Vive la nouvelle entente cordiale	220
Chapter 52.	USA – Bush fire under control?	223

Chapter 1. INTRODUCTION

Why This Book?

The origins of this book lie in a decision I took some years ago to start writing for policy-maker and practitioner oriented magazines. This was a very deliberate choice – I continued to write for academic journals and to write books but in the sure and certain knowledge that the former especially have very small readerships and mostly only in the academic world.

If, as social scientists studying 'government' – how it works, what it does and how it can be improved – we restrict ourselves to talking mostly only to ourselves we are clearly failing in one very important respect. Our subject matter does not belong just to us, it belongs to all citizens and especially those actively engaged in trying to make the state and public domain work better. We therefore have a duty, in my view, to share what we know and think with a much broader audience than those that read scholarly journals.

This is not an "either or" choice, but a "both and" obligation. Some of my social science academic colleagues still frown upon such 'engagement' with the real world and allege it inevitably weakens ones objectivity and distracts from serious research. They are not only wrong, but they have also clearly not noticed the proliferation of professors of "the public understanding of science". If the public need to understand the work of the physical sciences better, then they certainly also need to understand the work of the social sciences, and especially those relating to the role of the state, public services and the general public domain (Marquand 2004).

I found the process of getting into writing for a broader audience instructive – it requires different rhythms, construction and presentation from academic writing. Fortunately I had some expert guidance to get me started, especially my friends and colleagues Judy Hirst and Mike Thatcher of *Public Finance,* Nick Timmins of the *Financial Times,* David Walker of *The Guardian* and *Public* magazine, and David Allaby of *Public*

Servant – all of whom have taught me a lot about journalism either by example or direct advice (but none of whom are to blame for what follows).

This book is a collection of some of the outputs from that decision. I confess I was slightly taken aback myself when I started collecting this material together and realised quite how much I had written in this form over the past few years.

The justification for bringing it together is fairly simple: although it was published for much broader audiences (*Public Finance*, for example, has a weekly readership of tens of thousands) than any academic treatise, it would still have only reached a limited selection and is not easily available without a great deal of Googling. Most of my academic colleagues and friends will probably be completely unaware of what is in the pages that follow, for example. My main outlet, *Public Finance*, as the name suggests, goes mostly to financial specialists although it does reach a wider policy-maker audience too. So the aim of this volume is therefore to make the work available to a wider set of people.

However there is also a second and perhaps the most important reason for this collection and that is that the whole is, I hope, much greater than the sum of the parts. What the articles collected in this volume show is a consistent way of approaching and analysing change (or more often attempts at change) in modern public administration or "modernising government" as the early New Labour government of Tony Blair called it.

This collection covers a limited period – 2003-2008 – and I have written much more since then. In early 2009 I launched my 'Whitehall Watch' blogsite. This was partly born out of frustration at the slowness of traditional publishing and an eagerness to try something new. WW proved very successful with views rising from 13,000 in the first year to almost 55,000 by the final full year (2012) of publications.

Most of the articles published on WW between 2009 and 2013 are available on my new blogsite 'Public Investigations' (https://colinrtalbot.wordpress.com).

The rest of this introduction will spell out what I think some of those lessons and approaches are and ought to be.

The Public Domain Matters and is Here to Stay

This is a book primarily about innovation, inertia and ineptitude in British central government – although a few other institutions and governments get a mention too.

As Benjamin Franklin famously opined in 1817, "'in this world nothing can be said to be certain, except death and taxes." For taxes read government. In the 1980s it seemed that in some advanced countries a new wave of politicians, led most famously by Margaret Thatcher and Ronald Regan, were intent in making this statement a bit less true. They wanted to "roll back the frontiers of the state", cut taxes and reduce the public services that had grown up in most western societies, especially in the post World War II period.

The Thatcher-Regan revolution essentially failed to the extent that its aim was to introduce a much smaller state – three decades later the public sector, as defined by the relative amount of money it takes in taxes and spends on benefits and services, is on average about the same size, if not bigger, than it was in 1980 across the advanced OECD countries (OECD 2005). A few small states – notably New Zealand and Ireland – did significantly reduce the size of government, but most merely stabilised. This might be claimed as a victory of sorts – prior to this the state was mostly expanding and halting that expansion could be seen as a result of the Thatcher-Regan era – but it is not the one they promised.

Nevertheless real change has happened, and continues to happen, in how much governments do, what things they do and crucially how they do it. Whilst the monetary side of what governments do (tax and spend) has relatively stabilised, the regulatory side has almost certainly grown (again, despite rhetoric about de-regulation). But how public services – and which public services – are delivered and how they are paid for has changed.

On the finances side, there has been a big shift from direct to indirect taxation, which is arguably far less transparent – there is no line in people's pay slip about the amount of indirect taxes they paid last week or month, unlike income tax. Indirect taxes are also more likely to be at best flat and at worse 'regressive' – i.e. people on lower incomes can be hit harder, relatively, than those on higher incomes. They are certainly not progressive in nature. Progressive taxation of income was a policy shared, if differently enacted, by all major democratic political parties for most of the 20th century so a shift to indirect, non-progressive, taxation is major shift still all too often ignored in our collective fixation with income based taxes.

Back in the early 1990s when I was helping set up a research centre to study public sector management an academic colleague, who was herself fairly left-wing, asked why I was bothering as there soon wouldn't be any public sector left to manage. This was symptomatic of the mood at the time. Since then the *zeitgeist* has changed. Two emblematic and almost simultaneous events register the shift.

First was the publication in 1997 by the World Bank of their report "The State in a Changing World (World Bank 1997). This heralded a break with two decades of "structural adjustment" dismemberment of public activities in developing countries under the so-called 'Washington Consensus' - which was essentially that only markets mattered. Instead, the Bank now argued, the state and its institutions and public services, mattered too. This was a sea change in attitudes.

In the UK the second change emerged when Gordon Brown announced the first 'Comprehensive Spending Review' in 1998 (Chancellor of the Exchequer 1998), which contained the start of the first big expansion in public provision in the UK after the era of Thatcherism. What was significant here was the faith in public sector provision – the message was very clear – the public domain matters. This has now become so entrenched that as of 2007 all three main parties in the UK were committed to more-or-less the same level of public spending in the short term (i.e. they all adopted Labour's 2007 Comprehensive Spending Review's overall spending plans for 2008-2011). Even the Conservatives are committed to only a fairly modest reduction in public spending as percentage of national wealth, and not until after 2011, by 'sharing the proceeds of growth' between spending and tax cuts. This is a remarkable turn-around from the 1970s.

In 2008 it is easy to look back and see that all successful modern democracies include a significant public domain – if measured by spending it varies between about one-third of GDP up to two-thirds. Significantly 'emerging' nations, such as the Asian 'tiger' economies, having started with much smaller public domains are starting to drift towards these levels too. It is tempting to assert that significant levels of taxation and public spending are the price for modern democracy and a civilised society. So the public domain is with us to stay – now the debate has moved very firmly onto the terrain of how best to use it.

Talk, Decisions, Actions and Consequences

The really large-scale changes of recent years in the public domain has been in how services are to be organised, delivered and managed – at least in the intention of policy-makers.

For example, large-scale bureaucratic institutions have been 'unbundled' – broken up into smaller, more focussed, units often with greater-autonomy over some aspects of their working and some form of performance contracting, targets or monitoring (Pollitt and Talbot 2004; Pollitt, Talbot et al. 2004). Sometimes this split has been organised along 'purchaser' and 'provider' lines. It has also often involved a degree of competition between public agencies – such as schools, hospitals and universities – to provide services, and in some cases this includes competition from non-public, voluntary or private sector, providers too (as in health and prisons for example).

Many analysts have contended that as a consequence of some of these changes – and other factors – the power of states to get, spend and regulate has also become more diffused – upwards to supranational institutions like the European Union and downwards through decentralisation, devolution and the disaggregation of public bodies and more 'networked' services. Terms like the 'network society', 'the hollow state' and 'multi-level governance' have become fashionable.

Most of these analyses have been heavy on rhetoric and somewhat selective with the evidence. That there have been shifts is without doubt, how big these shifts are is something else entirely – and they have not always been one way. Take the issue of the unbundling of government or dis-aggregation – breaking up into smaller units – which dominated most of the 1990s. As we show below (Chapter 15) (and see also Johnson and Talbot 2007a) we have since seen a period in the UK of re-aggregation creating bigger – in some cases mega – public agencies such as the merged HM Revenue and Customs (formerly the separate Inland Revenue and HM Customs) and Jobcentres Plus (formerly the separate Benefits and Employment Service agencies). And some of the unbundling was more fictional than real in the first place. So the real picture is much more mixed and complex than is usually reported by commentators.

The organisation theorist Nils Brunsson suggests that the organisational change can be separated into talk, decisions and actions (Brunsson 1989). Talk is often very rhetorical in nature, presents a simple view of what was wrong with the past and what a new future will look like, shorn of too much contradictory detail. Decisions do not always reflect the 'talk' – they are often more pragmatic. Actions are even more likely to be distanced from the simplicities of the rhetoric of change, grounded as they have to be to some degree in complex, and often contradictory, organisational realities. Indeed it is perfectly possible for 'actions' to end up being the direct opposite to what 'talk' had declared as intention.

This categorisation applies equally well to change in public services policy, systems, organisations and management. Reform policies are often couched in overblown rhetoric. The most usual trick is to construct some 'straw man' representing the past – in which everything is bad – and then construct a future scenario in which everything is seemingly good. As Brunsson argues, we all know that the past was actually more complex, containing both good and bad elements and the future will be similarly complex. It may be better overall, but it will rarely be purely 'better'.

I would add a 'consequences' category to Brunsson's talk, decisions and actions. The intended consequences that do actually happen — all too rare unfortunately; the intended consequences that don't happen; and of course the all too frequent unintended consequences that bedevil many reforms. The latter are usually caused by the failure of policy to recognise complexity in the first place.

To take a concrete example from earlier reform efforts — the introduction of the "internal market" into the NHS by the Tory government in the early 1990s. This was launched by a White Paper called "Working for Patients" —as the 'talk'. However, study of the 'decisions' soon showed that this was not exactly 'working for patients' at all but rather a 'purchaser' and 'provider' split in which the 'purchasers were not patients but District Health Authorities or GP fundholders acting as proxies for patients. The 'actions' — implementation — of the changes turned out to be even less about 'working for patients'. At the time I was a patient in London and found the way the system was implemented meant my GP — the estimable Dr John Dunwoody, former Labour MP and ex-husband of Gwyneth — had less choice about where he could send me to London hospitals than before. In practice — consequences — most research showed that all the contracts, competition and marketing made very little difference to actual patterns of provision — a situation some colleagues rather pithily called "playing at shops" (Common, Flynn et al. 1992).

Time for a Change?

Another factor that is all too frequently ignored in reform processes is time. In a study we conducted for the BBC a few years ago we suggested a timeframe for change in public services (see Figure 1). This was meant as a rough guide but it makes the point that reform processes usually take much longer than politicians, or electoral cycles, allow for. Instead reforms have often hardly gotten past the first stage of changing inputs before they are superseded by the next initiative. In these circumstances it is hardly surprising that real transformational change to performance and services remains often elusive.

Figure 1 Changing Public Services

Phases	What is it?	Timescales
Changing Inputs	Resources devoted to a public service or bits within it	Usually 1-2 years to shift budget allocations in a marked way.
Changing Processes	How public services are 'produced'	Roughly 2-4 years to make organisational, process, staffing and other changes – maybe longer if large capital investment is needed.
Changing Outputs	What public services actually produce – e.g. hip operations; pupils being educated; etc	Roughly 3-5 as input and process changes work their way through
Changing Outcomes	The ultimate effects of public services in better health and education	Roughly 5-10 years, but in some areas even longer – e.g. changes in children's services might take decades to work their way through into patterns of adult health, education, criminality, etc.

Source (Talbot, Johnson et al. 2004)

If I were to sum up my approach in one word it would be 'realism'. Realism about the complexities and contradictions of any human organisation, and especially the massive and massively complex world of public services. Realism too about how easy it is to change these systems – or rather how difficult it is. And finally realism about the time-scales that are involved.

Let this be seen as unwarranted pessimism rather than realism and let me stress that I think public services can change and improve. But it takes time, patience and above all persistence and a realistic appraisal of the 'art of the possible' – something politicians ought to understand but all too frequently don't.

And Finally…..

Just to prove my own fallibility, not all the articles reprinted here stand the test of time completely. Some of the rather rash predictions have not come true. For example 'capability reviews' of Whitehall departments turned out to have far more bite than I expected. And Gordon Brown as Prime Minister has not moved as decisively to transfer power from the Treasury to Number 10 as I expected. But overall the analysis of the attempted changes in Whitehall and public services more widely stand up pretty well. But you, dear reader, are the best judges of that.

SECTION 1. WHITEHALL WATCHING

This section might have been called "Mandarin Watching" as it focuses mainly on the denizens of that rarefied strata of the civil service that sees itself the elite. And they are indeed elite, in several senses. Sociologically the senior civil service has opened up somewhat in recent decades but it is still predominantly drawn from public schools, Oxbridge and the 'fast-stream' entry system, especially at the highest levels. They are also undoubtedly often extremely bright with razor-sharp intellects. In most cases they are still what used to be called 'generalists' with extensive experience of various forms of policy and legislation-making.

They are also elite in that they form a sort of informal (and in some cases also belong to formal ones to) club. Attend any gathering of senior civil servants and it quickly becomes apparent that many of them have crossed paths, often several times, during fast moving careers that usually see them in a particular job for no more than 2-3 years at most (any longer is seen as a failure, still).

An interesting aside here is the prevalent use of cricketing metaphors – 'getting some runs on the board', 'close of play', etc. Although this has been slightly eclipsed by management-speak in more recent years, it is still pretty common-place (and a senior civil servant is more likely to be a cricket than a soccer fan).

The cricket metaphors come not just from enjoying that game – rather it is the similarity between cricket – the exchange of roles from the batting to the bowling side – fits so well the way civil servants may one day be 'batting' for a spending department and the next 'fielding' for the Treasury or another department. It also fits rather neatly with their role as 'serial monogamists' to ministers and governments (a phrase I've often used to describe their constitutional role). In this role they act as 'gatekeepers' to ministers, having privileged access themselves and able to deny it, or at least tightly regulate it, to others. They prize their role as the main policy advice givers to ministers, and are jealous of anyone else – like special advisers – who might get in the way of this.

Whilst the way senior civil servants are recruited and trained (mostly on the job with no further professional or academic training) provides for a culturally homogenous and tightly-knit corps, with finely honed policy-making skills, this has its obvious disadvantages.

Most senior civil servants have absolutely no experience of actually running a front-line public service, no experience in local government, education, health or policing. And it frequently shows in the way policies are designed with little thought to delivery – small wonder this is the area most strongly criticised in the recent round of departmental capability reviews.

Don't just take my word for it. Sir John Bourn, the recently retired Comptroller and Auditor General and head of the National Audit Office for 20 years wrote in the Financial Times (14 May 2008):

"My experience has taught me that fundamental improvements are urgently needed......The whole culture of the senior Civil Service needs to be changed. The top jobs should go to those who have successfully managed programmes and projects - in health, social welfare and taxation, as well as construction and defence. At the moment they are given to those best at helping their ministers get through the political week. Changing this would produce a new breed of civil servants, who would concentrate on securing successful public services. It would alter ambition and behaviour right down the line".

But it is not just the experience and training of the senior civil service that is problematic – it is the institutional and constitutional system within which they work. Being solely accountable to ministers – technically civil servants cannot even speak to parliament except as mouthpieces for 'their' minister – provides a shield against external accountability, especially by parliament. This situation of supposedly neutral (as opposed to politically appointed) civil servants solely responsible to ministers is almost unique amongst advanced democracies.

So too is the strangely powerful role of HM Treasury. During the Blair-Brown years the tensions between PM and Chancellor were invariably reported in purely personal terms – missing the fact that there has always been intense rivalry between the institutions of Number 10 (and the associated Cabinet Office) and Number 11, which long predated Messrs Blair and Brown and will probably long survive them too (Heclo and Wildavsky 1981; Thain and Wright 1996). The balance, at least in domestic policy areas, has clearly tilted towards Number 11 and HM Treasury during the past decade. Where it will go now remains to be seen.

These are some of the issues touched upon in the selection of articles that follow.

Chapter 2. Walking the walk

Public Finance 28-11-2003
Number 10 talks a good public service policy talk. But the real – and growing – power in Whitehall resides in the Treasury and this is not a healthy state of affairs.

Chancellor Gordon Brown is about to announce – rather later than usual – his annual Pre-Budget Report (HM Treasury 2003). In some ways, the PBR takes all the fun out of the real Budget, at least for people interested in how much the government is going to spend, tax and borrow next year. The actual 'Budget' in March is now something of an anti-climax. It has lost much of its impact on the markets because it only fills in the details. Everyone knows in advance the big picture from the PBR. And of course there are the Spending Reviews, which supposedly fix government spending plans for two years at a time.

As the PBR comes out, the cognoscenti will be reading the runes for several things. The economists will be looking at the Treasury's forecasts for economic growth. The financial markets will be eagerly looking at the estimates for government borrowing – is there really a black hole in the finances? Both will be trying to guesstimate the impact on the Spending Review announcement in June or July next year (HM Treasury 2004).

And the political commentators will be looking to see how Gordon is (allegedly) trying to upstage and/or frustrate Tony Blair this time. Finally, there'll be a bit of psycho-babble about whether the Iron Chancellor has melted into Cuddly Gordon now he's a father.

What will not appear in any of these discussions is the bizarre way we do these things in the UK compared with most other democracies, especially the central role that the Treasury plays. On November 17, the Treasury posted two press releases that were wonderfully symbolic of its changing role.
The first announced 'new measures enabling local authorities to create jobs, support business and promote enterprise'. Now what is strange about this is that responsibility for local authorities lies with the Office of the Deputy Prime Minister. Enterprise

policy is in the hands of the Department of Trade and Industry, which deals with businesses. Both of these are the spending and policy-making ministries one would think would be making such announcements, rather than the Treasury.

The second press release was the announcement of the new head of the Treasury's Public Services Directorate, Ray Shostak – the former head of Children's Services in Hertfordshire and, more recently, with local government's Improvement and Development Agency. The Treasury permanent secretary, Gus O'Donnell, welcomed Shostak, saying his 'direct experience of delivering public services will be invaluable to the Treasury agenda for improving the quality and cost-effectiveness of public services'. Note the words: 'the Treasury agenda' – such small slips of the tongue reveal a great deal about what the department thinks of its vastly expanded role in controlling policy developments right across Whitehall. From the ashes of losing its control of the 'commanding heights' of the economy, it has risen phoenix-like as the new arbiter not just of spending, but also of many policy issues.

The UK Treasury has always been a peculiar beast. Part-economics ministry, part-regulator, part-finance ministry, in the past it sat like a giant spider at the centre of a web of controls that ran throughout Whitehall and the country. Back in the pre-Thatcher era, these controls were formidable. In the economic sphere, the Treasury could fix interest rates, print money, buy and sell sterling, regulate credit, control capital flows and, through the host of nationalised industries, directly intervene in markets. In the public finances, it not only had almost absolute power to say 'yes' or 'no' to spending plans, but controlled pay and grading structures, settled pay and micro-managed spending departments' budgets.

On the surface, it may seem that the Treasury has lost huge amounts of power since those halcyon days, as indeed in some ways it has. Many of its economic powers were stripped away during the 1980s and 1990s by Thatcherism. In 1997, the final nail was New Labour's handing over the power to set interest rates to the Bank of England.

As the Labour peer David Lipsey has pointed out in his book, The Secret Treasury, this was always the 'sexy' end of Treasury activity (Lipsey 2000). Bright young macro-economists and suave civil service mandarins pulled the various levers at their disposal, or rather advised chancellors which ones to pull. Now these powers have vanished, there can never again be anything like the sight of a hapless Norman Lamont emerging into Downing Street to announce ever more ludicrous interest rate hikes, as happened during the 1993 Exchange Rate Mechanism crisis.

Over the same period, the Treasury made a bonfire of many centralised controls over the details of how the 'spending ministries' ran their fiefdoms and spent their money. Pay and grading were devolved (mostly), controls over programme spending and administrative overheads or running costs replaced them (and proved far more effective at controlling profligate ministries) (Talbot 1997).

Alongside this erosion of many of the Treasury's traditional roles and powers, there has been a perceived growth of a presidential-style prime ministership. Margaret Thatcher may have started, or some would say merely accelerated, the trend but Tony Blair has clearly made it his own. Over recent years, the more serious newspapers and magazines have devoted hundreds of column inches to the growth of a 'prime minister's department' in Downing Street, with the host of 'strategy units', 'delivery units' and czars for everything from drugs to cancer to rough sleepers.

So is the Treasury diminished beyond recognition, a faded image of its former glory? Has it suffered from a kind of 'descent from Heaven' (the wonderfully evocative phrase of the Japanese, used to describe the parachuting of top civil servants into senior jobs in the private sector)?

Far from it: certainly in the sphere of public policy and spending, the Treasury now wields greater power than ever. The powerhouse of public service reform may be in Downing Street, but if it is, it is in Number 11 not Number 10.

First, the reform of Treasury controls over the 'spending ministries' has strengthened rather than weakened its role. While it has let go of many micro-controls, it has put in their place much more robust controls over the spending 'envelope' for each major area of public spending. This happened largely under the Tories, but Gordon Brown's reforms – abolishing the annual spending round (PES) and replacing it with two-yearly Spending Reviews, introducing distinctions between annual and longer spending plans and reinforcing those between capital investments, running costs and policy spending – have all cemented this process (Chancellor of the Exchequer 1998).

What has happened is not – as some still suggest – some sort of simple decentralisation, but rather strategic centralisation and operational decentralisation. Spending ministries can, to use a rather hackneyed metaphor, rearrange the deck chairs but Captain Brown mostly decides – through the Spending Reviews – where the *Titanic* ship of state is heading.

Secondly, as the first press release cited above suggests, the Treasury has expanded its role into micro-economic areas. The reshaping of the tax and benefits systems to create incentives to work rather than remain on benefits has been the flagship of this approach. A symbolic organisational change was the transfer of the Contributions Agency from the Department of Social Security (mainly concerned with issues of welfare) to the Inland Revenue (the welfare to work agenda) and the merger of the Employment and Benefits services.

The national minimum wage has supplemented the tax credits with extra pay from employers, although the Treasury fought a rearguard action to mitigate its effects through restricting its level and exempting younger workers. Treasury action on competition policy has led to battles with Whitehall departments supposedly 'captured' by their 'client' groups (transport, industry and agriculture).

At the same time, it has led to deregulation policies, especially of labour markets, and re-regulation, especially in areas such as financial services. Productivity issues, including how best to encourage increased research and development and IT investment through tax incentives, have taken up a lot of time.

These types of policies have required a distinct shift from macro to micro-economic analysis. As a journalist friend put it: 'You used to be always tripping over macro-economists in the Treasury, now they're all micro-economists.'

Thirdly, the Treasury has ramped up its involvement in setting departmental objectives and monitoring their delivery across all areas of policy. The introduction of Public Service Agreements in the 1998 Spending Review (HM Treasury 1998), supplemented by Service Delivery Agreements in SR 2000 (HM Treasury 2002), means that, in effect, departments are being held to account not just for spending but also for delivery.

Fourthly, the Treasury has increased enormously its general micro-economic analysis activity on issues such as regulation and, especially, on evaluation of policies. The UK previously had a weak record on the latter but since 1997 has poured millions of pounds into a wide range of evaluation activities and has revamped the Treasury 'Green Book' guide to evaluation practice. The Public Sector Productivity Panel, another Treasury initiative, has churned out analyses of areas where improvements can be made.

Set against this, the powers of Number 10 are pretty feeble. The Treasury has its hands firmly on both of the purse strings and most of the accountability mechanisms for delivery, as well as having sucked in whole policy areas, such as welfare to work and regional economic regeneration. Its sense of superiority is undiminished. One insider commented to an academic colleague: 'They've got what, ten or 20 first-class minds in Number 10? We've got 200 in the Treasury.'

In most European and other developed countries, this sort of overbearing power – vested in what is effectively a finance ministry – would be unheard of. In the UK, it is compounded by an enfeebled legislature, which plays no role in public expenditure decisions, and the complete lack of transparency in Budget decisions.

The power of the Treasury is an unhealthy centralism in a pluralist democracy. It, in turn, produces centralism between Whitehall and town halls, schools, hospitals and the rest of the public services. The reason HM Treasury wants people like Ray Shostak, experienced in running public services, is not to help inform better public spending decisions but to help implement the 'Treasury agenda'.

Some fairly simple reforms could change this. Publication of draft Budgets and spending plans for widespread discussion, organised through parliamentary committees, would be a start. Voting on spending plans by Parliament would be even better.

In most democratic countries, the legislature plays a much more active role. The US is perhaps an extreme case, where the 'separation of powers' designed by the writers of the constitution deliberately **shares Budget-making powers** between the president (who proposes, through the Office of Management and Budget) and the Congress (which disposes, through its Appropriations Committees).

Even relatively recent democracies (in modern times at least), such as Greece, publish draft Budgets which are then subject to public debate before final authorisation. Ironically, our own Department for International Development spends millions of pounds promoting what is called 'participatory budgeting' in developing countries – something the Treasury would die in the ditches to prevent here.

Slimming the Treasury down into an actual finance ministry would help – moving some of its powers over regulation, enterprise and some other policy areas into the relevant ministries. And strengthening the role of what should be the centre of government – the Prime Minister's Office – would also move us in the right direction. As my colleague Professor Sue Richards puts it: 'You don't put the finance department in charge of strategy.' It is about time UK Plc realised this and put Parliament and the premier where they belong in a modern democracy – in charge.

Chapter 3. A hard Act to follow

Public Finance 06-03-2004

The issue of civil service neutrality and independence has been thrown into sharp relief by the controversy surrounding the Hutton report. Would a Civil Service Act help clarify matters?

In the furore over Lord Hutton's criticism of the BBC and exoneration of the government, some of the wider implications of the whole episode seem to have been lost (Hutton 2004). This has been compounded by Hutton's decision – criticised by David Kelly's family – not to make recommendations to ensure that 'what happened to David Kelly never happens again'.

Some say there could still be dramatic fallout in Whitehall, particularly now the government has confirmed there will be an independent inquiry into the intelligence that led Britain to war with Iraq. Official secrecy can never be the same again, they argue. A new Act to put civil service independence beyond question is more likely. And the Phillis review of government communications, which was also triggered by the Kelly affair, will curb the spin-doctors (Phillis 2004). At least, so some think. What will the reality be?

The three great Whitehall questions thrown up by the Hutton inquiry (Hutton 2004) were: What do you do with a whistle-blower when they are tangled up in a massive national political crisis? Should ministers have 'special advisers' and what is their role? How can the civil service (including the intelligence agencies) be both neutral and a servant of the executive at the same time?

Name and shame?

Prior to Hutton reporting, a great deal of comment was expended on the issue of 'who named David Kelly? Little ink, and still less grey matter, seemed to be engaged in asking the question: should David Kelly have been named, or rather why should he have not been named?

On this subject Hutton concludes: 'The government acted reasonably in issuing the press statement on July 8 that a civil servant had come forward to volunteer that he had met Mr Gilligan' (para 398). He adds: 'Whatever may be the position in other cases, I think that in this case it was recognised by the Ministry of Defence that because Dr Kelly's name was bound to come out and because the issue was one of great importance, it was better to be frank with the press and confirm the correct name if it was given' (para 409). In fact, Hutton even suggests that the only reason the MoD did not name Kelly themselves was that they were not entirely sure that he was Gilligan's source (para 409), with the clear implication that if they had been sure, they could have legitimately named him.

The key words above are 'whatever the position in other cases'. Hutton was forced into a pragmatic judgement because there is little but 'custom and practice' to go on. There are rules, in the sense of secrecy laws, freedom of information laws and some codes of practice, but these do not cover the specific case of naming (or not) a leaker (or any other civil servant for that matter).

The traditional position – in the era of 'Sir Humphrey' – was that civil servants should be neither seen nor heard. Over the past 20 years there has been a general opening up of the civil service and the exposure of various individuals during a variety of inquiries. Civil servants are much more seen and heard.

The creation of more than 100 'executive agencies', each with their own chief executive, accelerated this. It became fairly common for the chief executives to speak out on issues whatever the traditional rules said, for example, Michael Bichard (Benefits) and Mike Fogden (Employment) criticising 'market testing' in the early 1990s, and successive Prison Service director generals.

There have been several public and parliamentary inquiries in which individual civil servants have been fully exposed to public scrutiny. When appearing before parliamentary committees or inquiries, civil servants were (and still formally are) governed by rules that say they appear only on behalf of their minister and can say only what she or he allows – something few seem to have understood about, for example, David Kelly's appearance before the foreign affairs select committee shortly before his suicide and the ensuing controversy.

The position of those who leak information that is confidential and/or covered by the Official Secrets Act is even trickier. Can or should they be named? Here there are no rules to go by at all.

The nearest equivalent circumstances are Clive Ponting after the Falklands War and right now Katharine Gun, the sacked GCHQ translator accused of leaking over Iraq. Ponting's acquittal on a 'public interest' defence made Whitehall highly dubious about naming and prosecuting leakers unless absolutely necessary, as in the cases of intelligence officials such as Gun and Mark Shayler. Non-intelligence officials were more likely to be quietly sacked or demoted. Their anonymity was protected but more to maintain Whitehall secrecy than for their sakes.

We all know (now) what happened when Kelly was named. But what would have happened if the government had withheld his identity, if it had said: 'We know who Gilligan talked to, he didn't say what Gilligan said he said, but we're not going to tell you who it is'? A great clamour would have been raised, under the banner of freedom of information.

The real problem here for the future is how to create rules that protect public servants from exposure over 'personal' matters but spell out how far it is necessary to name them for public accountability reasons. The problem is where to draw the line?

A leaker who is prosecuted automatically gets named. What if they are disciplined and sacked (as Gun was at first and not named)? Or just disciplined or warned? And how important does their testimony have to be in setting the public record straight (as in Kelly's case) to justify naming? Many civil servants were named in the Arms to Iraq and BSE inquiries who had committed no offence and leaked nothing. Should leakers be treated differently and if so why?

Tough cases make bad laws. If the response to Kelly's suicide is a set of new rules that severely restrict the public right to know who a whistle-blower is, it would surely be a bad response and contrary to recent, welcome trends increasing Whitehall's transparency?

The special relationship

Alastair Campbell is the most well known of that supposedly new breed, the spin doctor. But the majority of Whitehall's 70 odd special advisers are, of course, not spin-doctors at all. They are politically partisan policy advisers, on temporary contracts, who come and go with their minister.

There is a great deal of muddle about the rights and responsibilities of these special advisers, their political masters and civil servants (including the intelligence services). Hutton was again forced into pragmatic judgements about the role of Campbell because there are no clear rules. He took the easy way out on this matter and simply wrapped Campbell's role up in the phrase '10 Downing Street' and discussed the relationship between the latter and the Joint Intelligence Committee and concluded that there was nothing improper (para 228). But this hardly clears up the special adviser's role.

The problems have more to do with the strange position of our civil service than of special advisers as such. Unlike in almost every other developed democracy, Whitehall mandarins are not governed by any formal constitutional standing or even legislation. According to the (famous or infamous, depending on your view) Armstrong Memorandum – the 1985 guidance on the duties and responsibilities of civil servants in relation to ministers drawn up by then civil service head and Cabinet secretary Sir Robert Armstrong – the civil service does not have a legal personality 'separate and apart from the government of the day'. The civil service is therefore not 'neutral' in a general sense but serially monogamous – it is attached solely to whoever is in power and has no wider public or parliamentary responsibility.

This distinction is important and is the fudge that lies at the heart of the 'British system'. Civil servants have always had to maintain a delicate balance between government and party – completely loyal to the first and 'neutral' about the second.

For politicians, when in power, the interests of government and the party are often the same thing. Special advisers fill the gap for ministers left by civil service 'neutrality' on party political matters.

But special advisers bring with them two problems, at least in the way we have dealt with the issue. First, they are public servants paid by our taxes and subject to civil service rules. This creates all sorts of ambiguities about their position, not least that they can be disciplined by 'career' civil servants (in theory anyway). Second, they have to function within the rest of the civil service, where many resent their very existence. Privileged access to ministers has been the most jealously guarded power of Whitehall mandarins – special advisers threaten that relationship.

The proposed Civil Service Act seeks to further clarify, constrain and entrench the existing position of special advisers. But it does not remove the ambiguities about their position, which is compounded by the other, much greater ambiguity about the role of the civil service itself.

In many other democracies, this conundrum is resolved by having politically appointed heads of various public services, who come and go with their ministers or parties. In some European states with perennial coalition governments, they even do this by quotas.

Getting in on the Act

The degree of muddle about the role of the civil service and special advisers and lack of clear rules flows directly from what the constitutional and civil service historian Peter Hennessy famously called the 'hidden wiring' – the obscure and usually opaque set of precedents, customs and norms laughingly called the British 'constitution', which is kept firmly in a closet somewhere in Whitehall. The solution being touted to at least some of this muddle is the Civil Service Act.

The public administration select committee has courageously drafted its own version in an attempt to force the government into action (Public Administration Select Committee 2004). Its draft is good as far as it goes, but that is not far enough. It mainly tries to codify what already exists and strengthen some rules governing the civil service and special advisers, rather than tackling more fundamental problems.

First, a Civil Service Act needs to form part of a much wider debate about the whole British constitutional set-up: the role of a second chamber and its appointment or election and how scrutiny should change; the role of a Supreme Court; and so on. The beauty of the US constitution – for all its flaws – is that its authors actually sat down and thought about the various powers of the state and how they might be balanced, including the role of the civil service. Their solutions might not be right for us, but at least everyone knows what they are.

Second, the proposed Act gives the civil service only a weak statutory basis. This is because it ignores the status of government organisations (ministries, agencies, etc). The UK is, again, almost unique in not having these arrangements sanctioned by the legislature.

Some parts of the civil service do have a statutory basis – the Inland Revenue and Customs and Excise, for example, with quasi-autonomous boards, rather like the BBC. But most Whitehall departments and agencies exist at the discretion of prime ministers, who can abolish, amalgamate and separate them at whim (and frequently do – John Major merged education and employment just to keep Gillian Shephard happy during his party re-election campaign). Parliament, not just the executive, needs to take a role in deciding what ministries and agencies we need to carry out legislation.

The discussion about whether the dossier on Iraqi weapons of mass destruction was 'owned' by the Joint Intelligence Committee (a purely civil service body) or the government was a classic example of this problem. Under current formal arrangements, it can be the property only of the government, however much everyone might want the intelligence services to be seen as neutral and independent (which in many ways they

are in practice). Hutton implicitly acknowledges this when he concluded: 'As the dossier was one to be presented to, and read by, Parliament and the public, and was not an intelligence assessment to be considered only by the government, I do not consider that it was improper for Mr Scarlett and the JIC to take into account suggestions as to drafting made by 10 Downing Street and to adopt those suggestions if they were consistent with the intelligence available to the JIC' (para 228, sect 7).
In other words, this was a government publication and, as such, a legitimate concern for Downing Street, so long as it did not distort the intelligence. But, yet again, this was a pragmatic judgement.

If we put the intelligence agencies (and the rest of Whitehall) on a proper statutory basis, like most of our European and our US friends, would these types of problems be at least partially solved?

Thirdly, the proposed Act ignores the distinction between civil servants whose primary role is delivering services – probably 90% of them – and the tiny but very important 'Whitehall village', which services ministers in their policy-making roles. A really radical solution might be to create a national public service separate from the civil service. This would incorporate all those involved primarily in service delivery – large parts of ministries, agencies, quangos, the NHS and even perhaps local authority workers – in a single framework of rules and responsibilities, with a public service commission. Whatever the solution, the current proposed Act does not address the question.
If Whitehall, the government, Parliament and the public are to learn one thing from the sad case of David Kelly, it ought to be that the age of 'muddling through' with our constitutional and civil service arrangements is long past its 'sell by' date.

Chapter 4. Bring on the professionals

Public Finance 26-11-2004

Are civil servants professional? The answer seems to be 'yes' when pontificating about policy but 'no' when it comes to actually running things. After the failure of Next Steps to remedy this, Whitehall is trying again.

In the 1960s and 70s, one of the bibles of senior Whitehall mandarins was a little book by a former head of the civil service, Lord Bridges (Hennessy 1990). Entitled *Portrait of a profession* (Bridges 1950), it contained his 1950 Rede Lecture in which he set out in no uncertain terms why the civil service was a profession.

For old Whitehall hands, it might therefore come as a surprise to see the headline 'Proving we're professional' on the Cabinet Office website. This announces an initiative by the Civil Service Management Board, launched on October 18, called 'Professional skills for government'.

Bridges went out of his way to make it clear he wasn't speaking about the whole civil service but only its higher reaches. His more politically correct successors claim 'a firm commitment to the idea of valuing every individual in the civil service as a professional'. But, in practice, the initiative is only about how people become top leaders in the civil service and has little direct relevance to the vast majority of its half-million-plus members who don't aspire to such dizzy heights.

So why the need for such an initiative 54 years after Bridges declared that the civil service was a profession, and why this focus now?

The various documents and speeches launching the programme claim that civil servants are already professional, but just need to become more so. But look at the detail and some of the 'between the lines' assumptions, and all starts to become clearer.

In 1988, the civil service started its biggest series of structural reforms since Northcote-Trevelyan in the mid-nineteenth century. This was the Next Steps programme of creating 'executive agencies' to run the operational end of Whitehall, such as prisons and the benefits, passport and tax offices (Jenkins, Caines et al. 1988; Talbot 2004).

'Next Steps' was built on the premise that previous reform efforts had failed to crack a simple problem. Whitehall mandarins' whole career structure and ethos were centred on policy-making and supporting ministers. They looked up at ministers, not down at the sprawling mass of services that central government provides, and which were consequently poorly managed. Executive agencies – with a whole new breed of operational managers – would solve this problem by effectively dividing the civil service in two: policy and strategy in the 'parent' departments and ministries; delivery in the agencies.

What 'Professional skills for government' implicitly admits is that this initiative has failed – or at any rate hasn't fully succeeded. The core of the new programme is to create three professional groupings in Whitehall: policy (headed by Brian Bender at the Department for Environment, Food and Rural Affairs); operational delivery (headed by Ian Magee at the Department for Constitutional Affairs); and corporate services, including finance, personnel, purchasing, project management, etc (no single head). These three groupings are meant to abolish the old 'generalist' and 'specialist' tags.

The key split here is between the policy analysts and the operational delivery people and the idea that there should be a 'parity of esteem' between them. The truth is that – as everyone in Whitehall knows – despite 16 years of Next Steps, the desirable jobs in Whitehall are still in policy, not operations, and those who have been promoted to the very top via the operations route are few and far between (one notable exception was Sir Michael Bichard, but he has left the service). Around 80% of senior posts are still located in ministries, despite the fact that 75% of civil servants work in agencies. The new programme is, in part, supposed to correct this but it is unclear how.

It will also, according to Sir Andrew Turnbull, the head of the civil service, provide 'a chance to recognise that professionalism is not the exclusive preserve of those disciplines where it is possible to earn letters after one's name'.

And here is the continuity with Bridges. The civil service has always been sensitive to the charge – most fully developed in the Fulton Report of 1968 (Fulton Committee 1968) – that its top ranks are staffed with 'gifted amateurs', generalists with no solid professional training. They might be good at 'policy development' and 'the conduct of government', as the accompanying brief states, but the more technical skills of policy analysis, evidence-based policy and strategy making, evaluation and research have not been their strongest point.

Since 1997, New Labour has spent hundreds of millions of pounds on evaluations and policy studies but one influential Downing Street policy wonk has admitted privately that most of it has been wasted. It is not hard to see why. Ironically, one of the proposals in the new scheme is precisely that 'a suite of accredited qualifications' should be developed for the three new professional groupings. So, apparently, you do need 'letters after your name' after all, at least if you want to be taken seriously as a profession.

Chapter 5. Cutting the Treasury down to size

Public Finance 28-01-2005

Slowly but inexorably the Treasury has been growing stronger. Tony Blair has made – and is still making – ineffectual attempts to wrest back some of this power. But perhaps only a PM Brown will be able to do this.

The chance of the Treasury escaping a radical assault on its power in the next couple of years depends on the unlikely prospect of the Tories getting elected. In a Labour third term, either Prime Minister Tony Blair or Chancellor Gordon Brown is likely to start dismantling some of its power. This might seem a surprising statement, especially in relation to Brown. But it is a possible, if not likely, outcome of the current situation.

Her Majesty's Treasury has always occupied a position of dominance in British public administration that foreign finance ministries could only dream about. As a combined economic and finance ministry, it has always been a bastion of power for whoever occupied 11 Downing Street. In recent years, its economic role has declined as other regulators (the Bank of England and a host of lesser bodies) have gradually taken over some aspects of economic policy and regulation.

Not everything has gone in the economic field – Brown's control over the supposedly 'economic' tests on euro entry attest to that. But what the Treasury has genuinely lost in economics it has more than made up for in other policy areas – especially social policy.

Brown has steadily shifted many aspects of social policy firmly into the Treasury's orbit. The integration of the tax and benefits systems (with the move of benefits from straight payments to various forms of 'tax credit') has been matched by a series of organisational consolidations. The Contributions Agency (previously part of Social Security) was absorbed by the Inland Revenue. Now Inland Revenue and Customs & Excise are merging into a new super-tax collector and enforcement agency. This gives the chancellor a whole battery of policy and organisational instruments to deploy.

The institution of Comprehensive Spending Reviews every two years, coupled with the Public Service Agreements demanded of every spending department, have further strengthened the Treasury's already overpowering role. As the ex-Treasury mandarin Sir Peter Kemp put it: 'All this might be tolerable if the Treasury were simply part of the centre, properly balanced out by Number 10 and the Cabinet Office. But that is not so.'

The Treasury has many of the real levers of power.
Blair has tolerated this accretion of power at the Treasury because it was both politically expedient and it seemed to work in driving through some fairly radical and redistributive policies (although no-one mentions the 'R' word). But, one way or another, the crunch is fast approaching.

If (when) Labour wins a third term, Blair is said to be thinking of ways of neutering the chancellor, the Treasury or, more likely, both. The most radical proposal is that Blair would slash the Treasury's 1,000 staff by 50% and move public spending and PSA control to a revamped Cabinet Office. This echoes moves by previous prime ministers, often for similar reasons – a too-powerful Treasury and a too-powerful chancellor.

All these attempts ultimately failed. The Department of Economic Affairs (1964-1969) and the Central Policy Review Staff (1970-1983) both eventually died.
Blair's attempts to balance Treasury power through a series of Downing Street and Cabinet Office units – the Strategy Unit, the Centre for Management and Policy Studies, the various public service reform units, etc – have all singularly failed to even slow down the accumulation of power in the Treasury.

Whether Blair could make such an initiative work this time is an open question. Certainly, with Brown still at the Treasury, that would seem at best questionable. With Brown removed, it might be more possible, but the systems he has put in place are deeply embedded and will be hard to shift. A much more intriguing question is – could and would Prime Minister Brown do it himself?

He has a strong reputation for being a hands-on minister – not afraid of policy detail and determined to have his way. Is it conceivable that if he were transplanted into Number 10 he would leave someone in Number 11 with the same powers and latitude that he has enjoyed? That seems highly doubtful – in which case PM Brown would set about moving the powers he had enjoyed in the Treasury from Number 11 to Number 10. And Brown – as one of the longest serving chancellors of modern times - knows where the Treasury hides all the bodies. He knows which levers it uses to have its wicked way with the rest of Whitehall.

If anyone could finally dismantle Treasury power and cut it down to size, it would be Brown. As prime minister, he would have both the means and the motive to want to see Number 10 and the Cabinet Office put firmly into the driving seat.
So whether it is Prime Minister Blair in 2005 or Prime Minister Brown sometime shortly afterwards, or perhaps even both one after the other, chances are that the Treasury is in for a hard time.

Chapter 6. Back to the future

Public Finance 04-03-2005

It is 25 years since the 1980s political satire, *Yes, Minister*, first hit our screens. But its portrayal of the senior civil service's success in resisting ministerial reforms is probably even more accurate today.

Two things happened last week which sparked the idea for this column. The first was that the BBC began a two-part series celebrating 25 years since the inception of the seminal — and terrifyingly accurate — TV series *Yes, Minister*. The retrospective is being presented by former Conservative leader William Hague from the point of view of Westminster and Whitehall insiders.

The second was a seminar organised by scholars from Queen Mary, University of London on 'outsiders in Whitehall'. It was attended by an interesting array of 'insiders' and 'outsiders' and a lively debate ensued — but under the Chatham House rule, so I can't say too much about it directly. I also do not wish to pre-empt the publication of the research. Suffice it to say, it has identified one or two 'problematic' issues.

But what both the rehash of Yes, Minister and the seminar raise (once again) is — do we have the civil service we want and need? There are several more straws in the wind that suggest this issue might soon be turning from one discussed mainly by Whitehall villagers and various Kremlinologists into something a little more serious.

The first is that the chatter from Downing Street is that 'delivery', or rather the lack of it, is still frustrating the prime minister. And it seems the civil service is being targeted as the principal culprit. New Labour wants, expects and needs to see dramatic improvements in public services — but another substantial increase in funding is not an option.

So someone has to be found to either make the extra cash work, or take the blame if it doesn't. That, in a sense, is one of the real political messages of the Gershon (Gershon 2004) and Lyons (Lyons 2004) efficiency and location reviews — 'Look, we've put up the money but the civil service has been wasting it. But we're on to them.'

The second is that the fallout from various inquiries — Hutton (Hutton 2004), Butler (Lord Butler 2004), Bichard (Bichard 2004) — has pointed to systemic problems with Whitehall which need systemic solutions. These issues are being doggedly pursued by the public administration select committee and others inside and outside Parliament. The issue of a Civil Service Act continues to rumble and a new 'Charter 88'-style campaign group dedicated to modernising the service is about to be launched — backed by significant media, academic and ex-mandarin figures.

The third is a negative indication. In recent months, three previous Cabinet secretaries (and heads of the civil service) have launched attacks on the government, blaming Tony Blair's style of running things for a variety of policy failures and crises. This is unprecedented and has to be caused by something. But what?

A charitable view would be that these high-minded public servants see a great wrong occurring that they feel compelled to right. More cynically, it might just be the old guard getting their retaliation in first.

Back in the mid-1990s, one of the three — Sir Robin (now Lord) Butler — was confident that he and the other mandarins had thwarted Conservative minister Michael Heseltine's attempts to introduce revolutionary change in the civil service — essentially by breaking it up. The two Continuity and change white papers, published in 1994 and 1995 (HMSO 1994, 1995), were seen as a triumph of continuity over change and their titles a sophisticated, if somewhat tongue-in-cheek, way of saying so.

All of this would not come as a shock to anyone who watched *Yes, Minister* and *Yes, Prime Minister*. In every episode, the mandarinate's ability to protect itself comes across loud and clear.

It is not that nothing has changed. Take the issue of bringing outsiders into Whitehall. There has indeed been a big increase in the numbers of people 'bought in' — but into where and to do what? In the heart of Whitehall, most of the outsiders are either ministerial policy advisers or in specialist units (like the 'drugs czar'). The experience of both groups has not been a happy one and, by and large, it is the advisers and czars who have departed with their tails between their legs.

There are more bought-in specialists in corporate jobs such as finance and personnel, but in the most senior ranks these jobs continue to be filled mainly by career civil service generalists.
There is also a whole layer of more professional hands-on managers in the executive agencies. But what is noticeable is how few of these make it to the very top — the mandarinate proper remains overwhelmingly career generalists, recruited as fresh graduates and schooled 'man and boy' (and now a few women too) in the ways of the Whitehall village.

So maybe we are in for a re-run of the Hacker versus Sir Humphrey battles so brilliantly portrayed in *Yes, Minister* — the first time round it was farce, this time it might just be reality come May 6.

Chapter 7.   If at first you don't succeed

Public Finance 25-03-2005

The trouble with most reviews and inquiries is that as soon as they report, their recommendations get farmed out and either float off or sink. Sir Michael Bichard bucked the trend by coming back to check on progress.

The Bichard Inquiry – into how the Soham murderer Ian Huntley managed to work as a school caretaker despite a long history of alleged sex offences – has just issued its final report (Bichard 2005). Confused? Didn't Sir Michael Bichard report last year?

Before I explain, allow me a small digression. In early 1997 – when Michael Howard was still home secretary - I received a phone call from a senior manager in the Prison Service. He asked if I would be prepared to serve on the Prison Service Review (de Frisching, Blairs et al. 1997), which was being established in the aftermath of the 'Derek Lewis' affair. Not really knowing what I was getting myself into, I agreed. The experience was instructive.

The then home secretary, Ken Clarke, had brought in Derek Lewis, a TV company manager, as director general of the newly 'agencified' Prison Service. Although Lewis had made a dramatic impact on Prison Service management and performance – including a substantial reduction in escapes – his misfortune was to be in charge when a couple of high-profile escapes from maximum security prisons happened.

The resulting political furore led to some of the most iconic moments of Michael Howard's career, including his famous grilling on Newsnight, where Jeremy Paxman asked the same question umpteen times, and Ann Widdecombe's 'something of the night' remark. Lewis was sacked (although he successfully sued for unfair dismissal) and, as part of Howard's 'not me guv' strategy, the home secretary announced to Parliament that he would order a review of the Prison Service. Everyone else quietly forgot about this obscure review (de Frisching, Blairs et al. 1997) – but not me, I was on it.

The review committee was consisted of three Prison Service directors, including Richard Tilt, the new DG; one representative each from the Home Office and Cabinet Office; Sir Michael Heron (then chair of the Post Office); and myself.

One of the first, and to me striking, things we did was to get a review of reviews – and we discovered that there had been no fewer than 14 over the previous 30 years. We eventually concluded: **'There is a striking repetitiveness about the findings of these reviews.'** The same problems had been identified over and again. There was rarely a follow-up of previous reviews, no continuity and no accountability for what they had – or mostly had not – achieved.

As in prisons, so in child protection. In January 1973, seven-year old Maria Colwell died after being horrifically abused. There was an inquiry. Thirty years and countless other inquiries later, another little girl's legacy was yet another inquiry – this time it was Victoria Climbié. As with the 14 reviews of the Prison Service there has been a sad repetitiveness about such inquiries. Lessons have certainly been learnt, and some even acted upon, but certain themes keep recurring.

Perhaps some problems are intractable, but one thing is obvious – once an inquiry issues its final report, it is up to others, often those whose systems have failed in the first place, to put things right.

All this came flooding back to me this week as I read the Bichard Inquiry Final Report (Bichard 2005) and a speech that Bichard recently gave about his experience of chairing the inquiry.

Bichard has clearly thought about the problem of inquiry follow-up and has done something unique with his own inquiry – he did not shut up shop after issuing his report. Instead, Arnie-like, he announced: 'I'll be back.' And he is. Six months later, he has come back to review progress.

The inquiry's first report (Bichard 2004) last year was fairly novel in not only making recommendations but also in naming which organisations should be responsible for implementing the changes he proposed. And it is those named who have now been asked by Bichard to account for what they have done.

The Home Office produced its own 142-page progress report for Bichard in December 2004 (Home Office 2004a). This detailed a veritable avalanche of activities. It is difficult to know what would be happening if Bichard had not announced his intention to come back, but it seems unlikely that things would have been pursued with quite such a sense of purpose and determination. In these circumstances there is usually dissipation as individual recommendations are farmed out, absorbed into broader work streams and either sink or float off.

Instead, a 'Bichard Implementation Programme Board' is busily at work and Bichard says he is 'impressed with progress'. There are two major projects that cause him concern, but the balance sheet is so far positive.

Time will tell if this innovative recursive approach has really made a difference. Bichard himself hopes that this will become a model for future inquiries. At a personal level, you get the impression that despite the inquiry now being formally over, he'll still be back from time to time. He used a loophole to do this – only the chair can close an inquiry. Let us hope that Whitehall's reaction is to build on this idea for others and not to try to close the loophole.

Chapter 8.   The more things change...

Public Finance 08-07-2005

The UK is unusual in having virtually no legislative control over central government reorganisations. Proponents of this state of affairs point to its flexibility, but it can also lead to flawed decision-making.

In my last column ('The ministry of silly changes', May 27) I suggested that it might be a good idea if government organisations – ministries and agencies – were put on some sort of legislative basis.

I was pleased to receive an immediate response from Sir Andrew Turnbull, the outgoing head of the civil service, politely disagreeing and saying that in his experience foreign visitors were always envious of the UK's flexibility in these matters.

We clearly talk to different people. In my contacts with international public administrators I find that many are shocked and frankly unbelieving when I try to explain the UK's remarkably non-legal basis for public administration. When I have been lecturing abroad on the Next Steps programme of agency creation in our civil service, people have flatly refused to believe there was no legislation authorising it.

So why and how is the UK different? Well, first it is not different in all cases. The supposed advantages of flexibility apparently only apply to Whitehall: local government, Welsh and Scottish government, quangos and many other public bodies are subject to legislation. Even a few bits of Whitehall are – the main ones being the revenue agencies (HM Revenue & Customs).

This is purely an accident of history, rather than by design. British government derives its authority from the monarchy, and ministries were traditionally established through Crown prerogative. Apart from the revenue agencies, where legislators insisted on a legal basis to try to keep the monarch out of the till, they never thought it sufficiently important to try to get control over what ministries and the government decided to create, merge, delete or – ludicrously, and sometimes purely vainly – rename.

This does indeed offer ministers more flexibility than they would enjoy in most other democratic countries. The churn rate in ministry structures is quite high. And one study in the 1980s, by Christopher Pollitt (Pollitt 1984), pointed out that these reorganisations tended to go in cycles – from small specialised ministries to super-ministries and back again.

But this rearranging of the deckchairs can be deceptive. It is mostly about simply redistributing functions. Few are abolished. Few are farmed out to local government or quangos, because that does require legislation.

Being able to carry out impressive-sounding but often fairly superficial reorganisations is certainly a political lever most governments and ministers seem to enjoy pulling. It creates a great impression that 'something is being done'. In some cases it is, and for good reasons. But there have also been numerous cases of vanity or spin-based renaming or reorganising, at great expense and with little benefit. And even reorganisations carried out for good reasons and in good faith but based on closed 'group think' in Whitehall have proved to be duds in practice.

There are good reasons why such changes should be subject to greater legislative restraints. The public service argument is one. Ministries are not just the creatures of ministers. They have to command widespread respect and have an ability to represent the public interest as well as the government's. To the extent that they start to be seen purely as creatures of the ruling party, they lose credibility.

The way most democracies resolve this tension between the needs of government and the need for a sense of public ownership is through legislative involvement in how public services are organised.

In the UK the position is weird – Parliament gets involved in authorising organisational choices only when these are away from the core. So MPs do get to vote on what non-departmental public bodies we have, or on how local government or NHS trusts and foundations are constituted but not on what the Home Office should do or whether we should merge Education and Employment, or split them up again.

In most cases these organisational issues are relatively uncontroversial but in some there are legitimate and important choices to be resolved. The danger of not having some sort of pre-scrutiny is that the executive will periodically make silly mistakes at best and dubious choices at worst.

The debate over the location of the Child Support Agency (stay at the Department for Work and Pensions or move to the new Revenue & Customs department) is a case in point. Parliament should have some say – uniquely in this case it would if it moved, because Revenue & Customs is based on legislation.

We do not want to end up gridlocked. But this can be avoided while retaining parliamentary involvement. In Tanzania and Jamaica, for example, a mix of enabling and secondary legislation has been used to push through agency-type programmes without unnecessary delays, but with scrutiny (Talbot and Caulfield 2002).

Chapter 9.   The thick of it

Public Finance 24-03-2006

The PM is to appoint a new independent 'ethics czar' to stem rising public concern over political misconduct. It doesn't go far enough.

What do the following stories have in common? Sir Gus O'Donnell, head of the home civil service and Cabinet secretary, is asked to investigate whether or not a secretary of state, Tessa Jowell, has broken the code of conduct for ministers.

Lord Butler, one of O'Donnell's predecessors, while giving evidence to the Commons public administration select committee, declares that ministers are frequently involved, sorry – 'consulted' – over senior civil service appointments. Butler again, in the same evidence session, criticises Parliament for its failure to properly scrutinise poorly prepared legislation.

Sir Nigel Crisp, permanent under secretary of state at the Department of Health and chief executive of the National Health Service, takes an early bath – sorry, an early retirement package – which includes a seat in the House of Lords. It is widely assumed he is being blamed, or taking the fall, for the financial crisis facing the NHS.

Finally, all hell breaks loose over the 'loans-for-lordships' scandal and accusations of election-funding sleaze.
The answer is a poisonous mixture of unaccountable civil servants, hypocritical and opaque conventions, prime ministers' draconian Crown Prerogative powers and our wonderful unwritten constitution, with just a dash of parliamentary disempowerment.

Let us review first the 'official' position. Under the UK's constitutional arrangements, Parliament is supposedly supreme (which is why it won't let anyone else judge MPs' behaviour).

The prime minister is appointed or dismissed only by Parliament. He or she appoints ministers who are also accountable to Parliament. The PM and her/his ministers in turn delegate some of their power to permanent civil servants (hence the 'permanent under secretary of state' title) to actually run things. So civil servants are mostly only indirectly accountable to Parliament and can speak to it only on behalf of 'their' minister. Still with me? Good, because now it gets complicated.

The PM is appointed not by Parliament but by the monarch. Of course, no modern monarch is likely to overrule Parliament unless they want to join Charles I. But monarchical appointment does have one big advantage for prime ministers – you get those lovely Crown Prerogative powers. No kowtowing to Parliament to get approval for ministerial appointments or chopping and changing departments, as the poor old US President has to do with Congress.

Civil servants' 'permanency' means that – officially at least – ministers neither appoint nor dismiss them. Otherwise, so it is argued, we'd go down a slippery slope and end up with a massive round of politically motivated appointments to senior public posts, as in the US. But how do you hold people to account when you can neither hire nor fire them?

So what's this all about? First, the ministerial code. Like its Da Vinci counterpart, it's a bit of a puzzler. It is authored by the prime minister of the day (although it's been around for a while, technically each new PM has to reissue it). It has no legal or constitutional standing and is authored, judged and sentenced upon only by the PM.

O'Donnell's role in the Jowell affair was purely to ascertain the facts and report to Tony Blair. We'll leave aside the fact that he has no way of ascertaining the facts other than to ask the ministers involved and accept his or her word. O'Donnell's role was carefully spun by Downing Street as having cleared Jowell, but of course he could not and did not do any such thing.
The truth is, O'Donnell refused to judge whether Jowell had broken the code, insisting that this was a job for the prime minister.

Blair has now accepted that the current position is untenable, and has issued yet another panicky response. To quote his official spokesman: 'The PM was proposing that an independent figure should advise ministers when they first came into office about any issues where there could be conflicts of interest. That same person should then be the person who established the facts for the PM, if there were any questions raised. The final decision-maker in that process, as the prime minister had himself stressed, should remain the prime minister.'

This new ministerial ethics czar would be 'someone who was genuinely regarded as an independent figure by the public and someone that ministers had confidence in regarding confidential matters', the spokesman added.

Second, let's look at Butler's statement that ministers are routinely involved in civil service appointments. While it is one of politics' worst kept secrets, it still apparently caused a sharp intake of breath at the PASC. Having Butler say this openly leaves a breach in the whole edifice of our conventions, which is that civil servants appoint civil servants.

The argument here has always been that if ministers get involved it will inevitably lead to the civil service's politicisation, an accusation first thrown at Margaret Thatcher for her infamous 'are they one of us?' question. The danger, we have always been told, is that we would end up with a US-style system of mass appointments every time the government changed.

But according to Butler, ministers are involved, and, if his evidence is anything to go by, over a wide range of appointments. This leaves us with a typical British muddle in which the official rules aren't clear because they aren't written down anywhere.

Third, and closely linked, is Crisp's departure. His whole history at the DoH – from his appointment as joint permanent secretary and chief executive of the NHS up to and including his departure – is a classic case of the Crown Prerogative's unchecked exercise.

In any proper democratic system, he would only have been dismissed by ministers (with an account to Parliament), or by Parliament itself, after due process and an open accounting.
Finally, Butler again. Who supposedly drafts legislation? The civil service, of course. For Butler to criticise Parliament for failing to correct bad legislation is a wonderful sleight of hand. He suggests that this is because ministers and their special advisers are running rampant, but where are the permanent secretaries – on 'gardening leave'? Yes, Parliament should be less supine, but whatever happened to civil servants 'speaking truth unto power'?

So what are the possible correctives to all these shenanigans? Perhaps a Civil Service Act, which settles clearly the powers and responsibilities of the service and, crucially and for the first time, makes them properly accountable to Parliament as well as ministers.

What about parliamentary adjudication on the code of conduct? How about the parliamentary appointment of the new ministerial ethics czar? Could we possibly have an open process for selecting and dismissing all senior civil servants, with an active role for Parliament? Don't hold your breath. After promising an Act, the government has gone silent.

A final thought. It is passing strange that what is right for foreign parts is definitely not OK for dear old Blighty. I am currently helping the UN Development Programme write a report on Macedonia. This small ex-socialist state is making valiant efforts to drag itself into democratic shape, helped in part by money and advice from our very own Department for International Development.

Some of the things they have been putting in place include civil service laws and legally binding codes for all manner of public administration activities.
Indeed, almost all the proposals suggested above are to some degree at least being implemented in Macedonia.

It is strange how we are willing to export principles that we aren't prepared to impose upon ourselves.

Chapter 10. Too clever for our own good

Public Finance 05-05-2006

'**At the Home Office, I worked with some of the cleverest and most dedicated people I have known.**' Thus wrote Katharine Raymond, a former special adviser to David Blunkett at the Home Office, in last Sunday's *Observer* (Raymond 2006).

The word that stands out here for me is 'clever'. After working in universities for the past decade and a half, I'm used to bumping into clever people and I've met plenty in Whitehall. But why is it that the main thing you hear constantly said about our civil servants – well the 'Whitehall Village' portion of them anyway – is just how clever they are?

Before having a closer look at this 'cleverness' issue, let's assess the size of the problem. First, the Home Office. It presides over the largest prison population in Europe and a re-offending rate for ex-cons of staggering proportions. It allowed illegal immigration to spiral out of control, disadvantaging genuine asylum seekers. Now it has presided over the worst possible combination of politically volatile elements – crime and migration – by allowing more than a thousand foreign nationals to walk free from prison when they should have been considered for deportation.

But let's be fair – it's not just the Home Office. The Department of Health has allowed the financial management and contracts of medics to get so out of control that over-spending has become a new flash point. How any department can turn the highest spending it has ever received into a crisis involving thousands of redundancies elevates 'cleverness' to new heights.

Indeed, all across Whitehall there are both the usual suspects – Ministry of Defence cost overruns and large scale IT failures – sitting alongside novel ones such as massive overpayments in tax credits to the poorest people (Revenue & Customs); even bigger failures to collect money off those who mostly can pay – absent fathers (Work & Pensions); failure to pay out to farmers

(Environment, Food and Rural Affairs); and finally an overspent legal aid budget leading to the loss of hundreds of jobs in the courts, and probably knock-on extra delays in criminal justice (Constitutional Affairs). The word 'shambles' doesn't even come close.

So, back to cleverness. A couple of years ago, an academic colleague of mine was discussing with a Treasury official how the department had amassed huge amounts of power under Chancellor Gordon Brown. My colleague believed, quite rightly, that 'you shouldn't put the finance department in charge of the organisation'. The riposte was again telling: 'We have 200 first-rate minds here in the Treasury – how many have they got in the Cabinet Office, 20 at most?'

Around a decade ago, I was present at the unveiling of a review of the Fast Stream, the mechanism by which bright young things are recruited from our top universities and eventually deposited in a permanent secretary-ship, with usually the minimum of frontline experience in between.

There was a fascinating exchange about what criteria you could use for selecting Fast Streamers. The report had concluded that testing for cognitive skills and intelligence was fine, but there was no point in testing for management ability as there were no such tests available.

This was slightly curious, I pointed out, as the government was at the time busily promoting something called the 'management competences' movement and there was a vast expansion in master in business administration degrees available. Somebody obviously thought you could both train and test for management ability. Our major employers were running such tests, through things called assessment centres, every day.

Many years ago, Meredith Belbin and his colleagues carried out a series of experiments with managers they were training. They gave them a battery of psychological and intelligence tests and then played around with various combinations of types to see which produced the best teams.

Their very first experiments were an enlightening failure. They selected those with the highest IQs and most outgoing personalities and put them all in the same teams. Over and over again these teams of the 'brightest and the best' failed to deliver. Often, they were so clever and so assertive individually that they could never reach agreement on what to do. Belbin concluded that effective teams needed a combination of different personalities and talents.

So remember, when the siren voices call for breaking up the Home Office, that just about every other central government structure has been involved in disasters. What they all have in common is not the structures, but that they are run by 'some of the cleverest and most dedicated people I have known'. How very true. It's time we realised running Whitehall really isn't rocket science, it's management – and they are not the same.

Chapter 11. An unholy mess

Public Finance 14-12-2007

Another day, another departmental disaster: can't the government get anything right? Colin Talbot takes an unseasonal swipe at civil service blunders – and asks what's behind Whitehall's annus horribilis.

The year draws to a close with the government in multiple crises, the Opposition Conservatives riding high in the opinion polls, against all the odds, and Gordon Brown's 'honeymoon' well and truly over. Given the Advent calendar-like daily dose of disasters that have befallen the government, it seems almost cruel to kick them while they're down. And in the season of goodwill too. But what the heck.

The attention of the media has been almost exclusively gripped by the high politics of the recent debacles. They have largely ignored the back story of a civil service machine that is tottering on the brink of catastrophic failure. Indeed, some would think it's already there. Just look at the litany of crises that are in whole or large part due to civil service failures.

In January 2007, we were greeted with the news that the NHS was headed for around a £1bn deficit, causing a slash-and-burn reaction in many trusts that were over budget. Although the ensuing cuts were relatively small compared with the massive increases of previous years the disruptive effect was profound.

By November, the £1bn overspend had turned into a £1.8bn underspend. Again this was small compared with overall NHS spending totals but in its own way just as disruptive and demoralising as the previous deficit.

In March, the environment, food and rural affairs select committee condemned former ministers and civil servants for the rural payments fiasco, which had cost farmers more than £20m in extra costs and the Exchequer a £400m fine from the European Union.

Also in March, the National Audit Office released its first report into the sale of part of the Defence Evaluation and Research Agency – Qinetiq – and the huge windfalls for the former senior civil servants who negotiated a lucrative deal that allowed the chair, Sir John Chisholm, to make a 19,000% profit – or £22m – on an investment of £129,000 (National Audit Office 2007).

In November, the NAO confirmed its original findings and issued a stunning rebuke to the civil servants who had let the top ten Qinetiq managers net more than £100m between them. The NAO concluded that the taxpayer could have earned many millions more from the sale and flotation if the Ministry of Defence had not been so incompetent.

In July, the NAO reported that the tax credit system had been defrauded by more than £3bn and had overpaid £6.6bn since it was introduced in 2003. Moreover, hundreds of thousands of people who had been overpaid had to pay the money back in circumstances that caused real hardship to the most vulnerable.

In September, the Child Support Agency admitted that in the previous financial year it had debts of £3.5bn, which had been increasing over the year at £20m per month.

And then, in November, Revenue & Customs lost two CDs. It could happen to anyone and the government immediately sought to blame a minor official. However, for the past couple of years, the Treasury select committee had been consistently warning that the combination of the merger of the Inland Revenue with Customs & Excise; the massive efficiency programme and job cuts; the failure to provide proper leadership at the top; and the somewhat reckless introduction of so-called 'Lean' techniques were piling up the pressure to the point where something could go very, very wrong.

Then there's poor Private Finance Initiative contracting; appalling IT schemes; messed up migration numbers – the list is almost endless.

And throughout this period we had the steady trickle out of the results of the departmental incapability reviews, as some unkind souls have dubbed them. These have shown remarkable consistency across Whitehall – they are all at best mediocre and at worst 'not fit for purpose' on any objective assessment of the results. However, in a recent response to the public administration select committee the government seems to have found the answer to this problem – reading between the lines it looks as if the capability reviews might be abandoned or watered down.

If it ain't broke, as the Americans say, don't fix it. But when it is palpably broke, the time is fast approaching where some serious fixing of our public administration is more than necessary, it is essential.

So why do we have these problems? There are numerous sources, of which the two principal ones are the essentially unreformed nature of the senior civil service and the, in some senses, over-reformed structures and systems.

As I have said many times before, our 'serial monogamist' civil service is almost unique in advanced democracies in having 'no constitutional personality separate and apart from that of the government of the day', as Lord Armstrong, the former head of the civil service, famously put it back in the 1980s.

In the dim and distant past, this did not stop civil servants 'speaking truth unto power', as long as it took place behind firmly closed doors. But with Margaret Thatcher's 'is he one of us?' doctrine, the already fragile autonomy of the civil service began to be dramatically eroded. Not by politicisation, as has often been alleged, but by managerialisation – the 'can do' mentality that when a minister says 'jump', the only correct response is 'how high, minister?' Serial monogamy has degenerated into serial subservience. In a highly centralised and adversarial system with relatively few checks on executive power, this is proving highly corrosive.

The result is that ministers can now launch just about any hare-brained scheme or re-disorganisation at the drop of a management consultant's hat. There is no-one to challenge them when they decide it is okay to merge two fundamentally different departments – the Revenue and Customs – and at the same time impose draconian efficiency savings, including massive job cuts based on staffing targets plucked out of the air. There is not even anyone to make sure that changes to the machinery of government, which come along with monotonous frequency, are at least made to work properly. The machinery of government group in the Cabinet Office was disbanded a few years ago. The new Brown government has taken this to ludicrous extremes with a set of ministry structures clearly built around the whims of various ministers with no analysis or thought.

Earlier this year, the PASC recommended proper parliamentary scrutiny of any machinery of government changes. Within weeks, Gordon Brown came into Number 10 and promulgated yet another round of Whitehall musical chairs without so much as a nod at Parliament – the same Parliament he claims to want to empower more.

Unless the civil service is put on a statutory basis, with clear autonomy and accountability, this will persist. Unless it is subjected to radical personnel reform that ensures policy mandarins have some real-world experience of delivering public services, civil servants will continue to give ministers policy advice that is often naïve and unrealistic and fail to challenge their more ridiculous ideas. The late US scholar Larry Terry called this the 'conservator' role of public servants – sometimes having to protect the integrity of public institutions against the wilder excesses of democratically elected leaders.

Let's end this unseasonal romp around the failures of Whitehall with a tale of what I call the 'Sellafield' ploy. I went to a secondary school in Barrow-in-Furness and just up the coast there was the largest nuclear facility in the UK – Windscale. It's not there any more – or rather it is, but now it's called Sellafield, part of the unexpected fallout from the Chernobyl nuclear disaster.
This year, we have seen one of the smartest uses of the Sellafield ploy I have seen in a long time. In July, the *Guardian* ran a front-page story headed 'Public sector targets to be

scrapped' (Carvel 2007). What followed was a masterful piece of spin in which Andy Burnham, chief secretary to the Treasury under the new Brown premiership, announced that Public Service Agreements were to be slashed from 110 to 30 in the forthcoming Comprehensive Spending Review.

Last week, the Treasury select committee published its report on CSR07 (HM Treasury 2007). They accept that PSAs have indeed been reduced to 30. But they also note that these 30 PSAs only replace a similar number of 'cross-cutting' PSA targets in the previous 2004 spending review (HM Treasury 2004). The 'departmental' PSAs have indeed gone – at least in name. Instead, there are now around 100 departmental strategic objectives.

To the untrained eye, these DSOs might look remarkably like the PSA targets they have replaced, with due allowance for a certain amount of churn, which has happened at every spending review. But no, according to the Treasury, these new DSOs are in some mysterious way fundamentally different to the previous departmental PSAs. Otherwise, the government would now have 'reduced' PSAs from 110 in 2004 to around 130 in 2007.

So DSOs are different, and Windscale is Sellafield and I still believe in Santa Claus. Merry Christmas.

SECTION 2. STRUCTURAL ADJUSTMENTS

One of the favourite activities of Ministers in British government is re-arranging Whitehall. It is the quickest way of showing that "something is being done" about a policy area, whether it be to address a problem or promote some new policy.

Or at least it appears the quickest. Setting up a new organization, merging and splitting old ones, or merely re-allocating responsibilities between two or more agencies takes time – putting up a new name plate doesn't. So it is easy to create the appearance of action where none, or little, has taken place.

As the articles in this section demonstrate, the temptation to "re-dis-organize', as it is sometimes known, is especially strong in British government for a simple reason – because they can.

Apart from a few exceptions (like HM Revenue and Customs) most Whitehall departments have no statutory basis – a position that is almost unique amongst advanced democracies. Most countries government Ministries exist on an explicit legal basis – either Constitutional or legislative – but not Britain's.

Although Parliament has to ratify changes to Ministries, this is almost always done long after the changes have already been implemented rendering Parliament impotent. Very rarely are major structural changes subject to any scrutiny before they happen and they are almost never evaluated afterwards either.

Some see this as a 'good thing' – witness the response I got from then (Sir, now Lord) Andrew Turnbull – the then head of the Civil Service - when I criticised this state of affairs. I'll leave you to judge for yourselves who's right.

Chapter 12. What's in a name

Public Finance 29-10-2004

Whatever happened to the Civil Service College? Find out in the first of a monthly column focusing on the mysteries and machinations of the government in action across Whitehall and Westminster.

Do the letters 'CMPS' mean anything to you? The 'Centre for Modern Psychoanalytic Studies' maybe? Or the slightly worrying 'Central Minnesota Practical Shooters'? No, the CMPS we are interested in is the 'Centre for Management and Policy Studies', part of the Cabinet Office. One is apparently no longer supposed to refer to it by its actual name but only by its initials — something about 'branding' supposedly. So what is it?

Well, effectively it is the once and future Civil Service College, located mainly on a beautiful campus-style site in Sunningdale. The story of how it migrated from being a slightly worthy institution into the shiny new Centre for Management and Policy Studies and back to being really just the CSC by another set of initials is a symbolic tale. It is an excellent subject for the first of these new columns as yet another failed attempt to create some 'central intelligence' in government.

In the early 1990s, the then deputy prime minister, Michael 'Hezza' Heseltine, embarked on a spate of privatisations of civil service executive agencies. Plans to sell off the Civil Service College excited a special interest. The college was, for Whitehall mandarins, part of the 'glue' that holds the civil service together, maintaining a sense of identity in a service being broken up into dozens of executive agencies (indeed, the college itself was made into an agency).

Hezza failed and senior civil servants openly boasted about having said: 'No, deputy prime minister'. The preservation of the college – together with some other changes, such as the institution of the 'Senior Civil Service' in the 1994 white paper Continuity and change (HMSO 1994, 1995) – were hailed as having protected the core of the civil service.

This core – the 3,000-5,000 people who do the policy work in the Treasury, Cabinet Office and spending ministries – all knew each other, often went to the same (private) schools and universities (Oxbridge), trained and worked together and moved around Whitehall frequently. It was this intense networking and socialisation that formed what a couple of analysts memorably called the 'Whitehall Village', and the college played an important role in sustaining this.

But despite this, governments have complained of a lack of central direction and co-ordination. Successive Prime Ministers have sought to create a unified policy centre under their control to replace the decentralised power of spending ministries and the alternative power centre in the Treasury.

New Labour was no exception when it came to power in 1997. One result, after much cogitation, was the Centre for Management and Policy Studies. At its core was the rescued Civil Service College, but its main purpose was to become a powerhouse for policy-making excellence and co-ordination across government. It would be linked, crucially, to the Cabinet Office and prime minister rather than the Treasury.

A leading academic, Professor Ron Amman, the former head of the Economic and Social Research Council, was brought in to oversee the combined policy centre and college. Great plans were laid and much fanfare devoted to it.

However, right from the start it was clear it wasn't going to work. Ministerial leadership was weak. The Treasury was busy amassing new powers over social policy (via tax credits and suchlike) and other policy (via the Comprehensive Spending Reviews). Spending ministries were reluctant to have yet another central unit second-guessing their policy making.

Even within the Cabinet Office, other policy units such as the powerful Performance and Innovation Unit, later renamed the Strategy Unit, remained aloof from the CMPS. A rescue attempt – putting leading modernising mandarin Sir David Omand in charge as 'chair' (a role created especially for him) – failed when Omand was whipped away after 9/11 to head security co-ordination.

So what is left of the grand scheme for a policy powerhouse? Well, not a lot. The CMPS has reverted to being essentially the old college under a new name, or rather new acronym. Its strategic direction, under the leadership of a human resources professional brought in from the private sector, seems purely training and development oriented. It has even lost its 'executive agency' status and been taken back into the Cabinet Office. All that remains of the 'policy powerhouse' is a useful 'Policy Hub' website which provides advice and a clearing house for policy ideas.

Number 10 has increased its own supply of policy advisers and the Strategy Unit achieved some success in real critical and strategic policy thinking (although the departure of its head Geoff Mulgan puts even that in doubt). The Treasury goes from strength to strength in garnering new areas of policy under its ever-expanding arms, but without an explicit policy function.

The fate of the CMPS illustrates once again that Whitehall is great at changing the names, but all too often the essential structures and processes of the Whitehall Village remain much the same.

Chapter 13. The ministry of silly changes

Public Finance 27-05-2005

Britain is the only major democracy whose ministries have no constitutional basis. This allows prime ministers to chop and change them at will, often in response to political power plays. It has to stop.

Announced in the post-election Cabinet reshuffle, the Department for Productivity, Energy and Industry – formerly the Department of Trade and Industry – must hold the record for the shortest-lived government department name in British history.

The name change was greeted with widespread derision and the DTI title was reinstated within days. The term 'Whitehall farce' springs to mind.

This is not the first time that the DTI has suffered name shame.

It used to be, in the grand old days, called the Board of Trade. In the early 1990s, Michael Heseltine produced much mirth when, taking over as DTI secretary, he announced that he wished to retain the title of 'president of the Board of Trade'.

What the DPEI fiasco tells us, however, is something rather more serious about how British government is run. It highlights a fundamental and serious quirk in the way we do things. Perhaps a rather more serious episode helps to bring this out.

John Major made history by standing down as leader of the Conservatives in 1995 and inviting his eurosceptic critics to oppose him in the ensuing internal Tory Party election. Immediately after his re-election, the departments for Education and Employment were suddenly merged under Gillian Shephard. Indeed, it was so sudden that one of the permanent secretaries involved was told about the merger only 15 minutes before the press conference to announce it.

Why this happened was a subject of much speculation, but the main explanation advanced was that Shephard had demanded the merging of the two departments under her control as her price for openly backing Major's re-election. Be that as it may, the real question was not why it happened but how could it?

The UK is unique among advanced democracies (and most others too) in having no formal legal or constitutional basis for our ministries. They can be created, merged or destroyed at the whim of the prime minister of the day, using their 'prerogative' powers. In other countries, primary legislation or even constitutional amendments – at the very least, secondary legislation – are needed before such changes can be implemented.

Defenders of our system would say it is far more flexible and adaptable, making it easy for the executive to get on with the job. Opponents would point out that unchecked executive power has a habit of producing policy and administrative disasters – the poll tax being a good example.

There are plenty of examples of power plays between ministers being the sole basis for ill-thought-out and sometimes simply bonkers changes to the 'machinery of government'. British government is littered – far more than most – with failed experiments in reorganising ministries as the solution to supposed policy problems at best, and to satisfy low political intrigue at worst.

The current situation has been exacerbated by a small and completely unremarked change Labour made some time ago – it abolished the 'machinery of government group' in the Cabinet Office. These were the people who kept all the lists of government functions and where they were located and why. When prime ministers wanted to make swift and secret preparations for a big change, this group did all the backroom work.

While this system was still arbitrary, it at least had the merit of being well organised – something that cannot be said of recent attempts at deck-chair rearrangement in Whitehall.

The reason that ministers, and especially the prime minister, treat the organs of state in such a cavalier way is simple – it is because they can. There are no checks and balances, no separation of powers, no authorisation required from the legislature to enable some scrutiny of these decisions. The civil service and its organisations (ministries) have 'no constitutional personality separate and apart from that of the government of the day', in the famous words of Lord Armstrong when he was head of the service. They are the playthings of ministers, full stop.

That might have been acceptable in an era where the civil service was mainly the private offices of ministers, although even that is doubtful. In today's world, where the bulk of it is employed to run big public services, surely the idea that these are only the creatures of the executive is nonsense? Public services are just that – public – and ought surely to be subject to a more balanced set of governance arrangements than just untrammelled executive power?

And the upside for government of a more formalised, balanced and scrutinised procedure for changing the machinery of government? Maybe they would have fewer disasters like the DPEI farce.

Chapter 14. The more things change

Public Finance 7 Jul 05

The UK is unusual in having virtually no legislative control over central government reorganisations. Proponents of this state of affairs point to its flexibility, but it can also lead to flawed decision-making

The UK is unusual in having virtually no legislative control over central government reorganisations. Proponents of this state of affairs point to its flexibility, but it can also lead to flawed decision-making

In my last column ('The ministry of silly changes', May 27) I suggested that it might be a good idea if government organisations — ministries and agencies — were put on some sort of legislative basis.

I was pleased to receive an immediate response from Sir Andrew Turnbull, the outgoing head of the civil service, politely disagreeing and saying that in his experience foreign visitors were always envious of the UK's flexibility in these matters.

We clearly talk to different people. In my contacts with international public administrators I find that many are shocked and frankly unbelieving when I try to explain the UK's remarkably non-legal basis for public administration. When I have been lecturing abroad on the Next Steps programme of agency creation in our civil service, people have flatly refused to believe there was no legislation authorising it.

So why and how is the UK different? Well, first it is not different in all cases. The supposed advantages of flexibility apparently only apply to Whitehall: local government, Welsh and Scottish government, quangos and many other public bodies are subject to legislation. Even a few bits of Whitehall are — the main ones being the revenue agencies (HM Revenue & Customs).

This is purely an accident of history, rather than by design. British government derives its authority from the monarchy, and ministries were traditionally established through Crown prerogative. Apart from the revenue agencies, where legislators insisted on a legal basis to try to keep the monarch out of the till, they never thought it sufficiently important to try to get control over what ministries the government decided to create, merge, delete or — ludicrously, and sometimes purely vainly — rename.

This does indeed offer ministers more flexibility than they would enjoy in most other democratic countries. The churn rate in ministry structures is quite high. And one study in the 1980s, by Christopher Pollitt, pointed out that these reorganisations tended to go in cycles — from small specialised ministries to super-ministries and back again.

But this rearranging of the deckchairs can be deceptive. It is mostly about simply redistributing functions. Few are abolished. Few are farmed out to local government or quangos, because that does require legislation.

Being able to carry out impressive-sounding but often fairly superficial reorganisations is certainly a political lever most governments and ministers seem to enjoy pulling. It creates a great impression that 'something is being done'. In some cases it is, and for good reasons. But there have also been numerous cases of vanity or spin-based renaming or reorganising, at great expense and with little benefit. And even reorganisations carried out for good reasons and in good faith but based on closed 'group think' in Whitehall have proved to be duds in practice.

There are good reasons why such changes should be subject to greater legislative restraints. The public service argument is one. Ministries are not just the creatures of ministers. They have to command widespread respect and have an ability to represent the public interest as well as the government's. To the extent that they start to be seen purely as creatures of the ruling party, they lose credibility.

The way most democracies resolve this tension between the needs of government and the need for a sense of public ownership is through legislative involvement in how public services are organised.

In the UK the position is weird — Parliament gets involved in authorising organisational choices only when these are away from the core. So MPs do get to vote on what non-departmental public bodies we have, or on how local government or NHS trusts and foundations are constituted but not on what the Home Office should do or whether we should merge Education and Employment, or split them up again.

In most cases these organisational issues are relatively uncontroversial but in some there are legitimate and important choices to be resolved. The danger of not having some sort of pre-scrutiny is that the executive will periodically make silly mistakes at best and dubious choices at worst.

The debate over the location of the Child Support Agency (stay at the Department for Work and Pensions or move to the new Revenue & Customs department) is a case in point. Parliament should have some say — uniquely in this case it would if it moved, because Revenue & Customs is based on legislation.

We do not want to end up gridlocked. But this can be avoided while retaining parliamentary involvement. In Tanzania and Jamaica, for example, a mix of enabling and secondary legislation has been used to push through agency-type programmes without unnecessary delays, but with scrutiny.

Chapter 15. Red tape and chaos theory

Public Finance 07-10-2005

At first sight, the plan to cut down the public sector inspectorates from 11 to four seems sensible. But a closer look shows there is method in the seeming madness of the current messy, overlapping system.

At the time of this year's Budget, the chancellor made great play of a decision to simplify audit and inspection in the public sector as part of his crusade against red tape and bureaucracy. In parallel with his efficiency drive to save £21.5bn, he promised to reduce the 'regulatory burden' in the public sector by cutting the number of inspectorates from 11 to four.

As usual with Gordon Brown's announcements, the detail turns out to be slightly less clear than the headlines. The best way of teasing this out is to look at the actual proposals for amalgamations. The biggest is to reduce from five to one the inspectors of the criminal justice system, merging those for the police, probation, prisons, courts and Crown Prosecution Service into a single super-inspectorate.

It seems sensible enough, you might think – why have all these separate inspectorates? But hang on a minute. These aren't separate inspectors inspecting the same thing, they are separate inspectors inspecting different things. While prisons and probation might be (sort of) merging through the National Offender Management Service, the other three are all distinct functions with different roles and responsibilities.

There might be economies of scale from putting all five inspectorates under one roof, where they could share back-office services, but it is hard to see the advantage in merging their core task of inspecting.

Checking up on prisons, police, probation, courts and prosecutors requires some in-depth understanding of each of these functions, and how they might be able to hide anything inconvenient. As we know from some of the spectacular failures of private sector audit, hiding bad stuff can be ridiculously easy.

Although there are some generic detection and evidential skills that apply to all inspections – whether hospitals, schools or prisons – there is also an important element of specialised knowledge that usually only comes from years of experience of a particular sector.

That is why we had specialist inspectorates – often drawing heavily on experienced practitioners in the field for their inspectors – in the first place. While this approach has dangers, it clearly has the advantage of having 'poachers turned gamekeepers' doing the inspecting.

It is true that some of the other amalgamations reflect the closer integration of the services they are inspecting – health and adult social services, for example, and education, children's services and skills. But these still contain an element of specialised knowledge needed to inspect specific services, knowledge that could get lost in the new 'super' inspectorates.

There is another issue here though – is coherent, joined-up scrutiny of a single public service axiomatically a 'good thing'? This is at least debatable, although there seems very little appetite from politicians, service leaders or inspectors to discuss it. The counter-arguments are, however, quite powerful.

Most public services – especially those delivering what the Americans call 'human' services, such as health, education and social services – are complex. The 'production process' is rarely simple and the products and outcomes difficult to pin down.
In these circumstances, having unequivocal, objective evidence about what is 'good' and 'bad' performance is problematic. We can gather plenty of evidence but it rarely 'proves' anything incontestably. It can be very useful fuel for discussion, but it often raises more questions than it answers.

This is why having multiple forms of inspection – not necessarily coherently co-ordinated and amassing comparable evidence – might actually be a 'good thing'. In that hackneyed phrase, it might just bring some checks and balances into the system.

This is what Professor Christopher Hood, director of the Public Services Programme, calls 'contrived randomness' in inspection (Hood 1998). The best analogy is with educational examinations. Candidates have acquired (we hope) large and complex bodies of knowledge and we can't possibly hope to test for all of it. So instead we ask them a few, seemingly random, questions about bits of it in the hope this will tell us how much they have learnt.

Maybe a bit of chaos in inspection might indeed be the very best thing for trying to pin down the complex and elusive performance of some public services. There are likely to be fewer places to hide bad practices than in a well-ordered, and hence predictable, inspection regime.

Chapter 16. Big is beautiful (again) – with Carole Johnson

Public Finance 06-01-2006

What goes around comes around. For decades, small-scale government was all the rage. Now large centralised public agencies are back in fashion. Colin Talbot and Carole Johnson investigate the merger mania that is leading public services to grow like topsy.

The 1980s and 1990s were the decades of the drive for small government. For most reformers, such as Margaret Thatcher, this meant less public spending, fewer people employed in the public sector and less regulation. On just about every count they failed. A major survey this year by the Organisation for Economic Co-operation and Development, Modernising government – the way forward (Curristine and Matheson 2005), concluded: 'Government has a larger role in the societies of the OECD countries than two decades ago.'

Public spending remained stubbornly around the same levels, as a percentage of gross domestic product, and even increased in some countries. Public sector employment did shrink slightly, mainly due to privatisation and contracting out, but remained at historically high levels. Regulation, though rather more difficult to measure, was commonly agreed to have increased, despite vigorous efforts to reduce it.

But small government also came to mean – especially in the UK in the 1990s – small organisations. It was the era of 'unbundled government'. Small, it seemed, was beautiful. Large, monolithic public services were to be broken up into lots of itty-bitty 'agencies': executive agencies in government, NHS trusts, locally managed schools, independent higher and further education institutions and so on. Hundreds of new organisations were hacked, sometimes brutally, out of the old public administration bureaucracies. They sprang up almost overnight, most with their very own chief executive, mission statement and designer logo.

Some academics attributed this movement to a global trend towards 'small-scale production' and the end of 'Fordist' mass production in both the public and private sectors. Others talked about the networked society or 'post-bureaucracy'. One recent award-winning business book by John Roberts (Roberts 2004) – The Modern Firm – discusses at length the new dominant model of the 'disaggregated' company. Later the change was attributed to the rise of a new 'managerialist' ideology and the so-called 'new public management'. This, in turn, was said to be fed by new ideas from economics – public choice, new institutional economics, transaction economics and so on.

The more pragmatic reasons given for these changes were many and various. Greater autonomy would give managers more room to manage. Organisations could focus on a single 'job to be done' rather than being large, one-size-fits-all, multifunctional monoliths. They would be 'closer to the customer' and more focused on their needs; as 'arm's-length' organisations, they could be managed through 'contracts' that specified their tasks, budget and performance. Multiple organisations producing the same services would enable the introduction of some form of competition between them. Finally, competition, contracts and more flexible management would between them produce efficiency savings.

All of these explanations seem plausible at face value. But, as the late, great, economics professor and Nobel Prize winner Herbert Simon pointed out in 1945, these sorts of maxims usually have exact opposites, which seem equally attractive. Managers need to be controlled to prevent them indulging in budget-maximisation and other games. Organisations too narrowly focused on the job-to-be-done can ignore the bigger picture and end up causing more problems than they solve. Public organisations have to safeguard the citizens' and taxpayers' interests by ensuring equity and sticking to the rules. Internal management is usually cheaper and more flexible than contracting out – 'make not buy'. Joined-up government is needed, whereas competition might lead to inefficiencies through wasteful duplication, unused capacity, extra transaction costs and poor co-ordination. Large-scale organisation is relatively efficient and offers economies of scale. Why duplicate back-office services and purchasing and supply when you can run them together?

Over the past 15 to 20 years, the first set of arguments has dominated policy. In 1995, the average public servant would have been working in an organisation that was much smaller than in 1985. But by 2005 the trend seems to be in reverse.

Today, a public servant is more likely to be working in a much bigger organisation than they would have been a decade ago. As the box overleaf illustrates, we are being engulfed by merger mania across the public sector.

In health in the early 1990s, for example, there was a massive disaggregation of the monolithic health service into 'purchasers' and 'providers' – the latter being mainly newly created NHS trusts. Initially, there was more or less one trust per hospital, but gradually throughout the late 1990s there was a series of mergers into ever-bigger trusts, now more usually involving four or five or even more hospitals. In some cases, the new super-trusts are as big as the old district health authorities they were carved from.

With local government and other services, there has been a similar trend. While some services have been given their independence – the old polytechnics, further education colleges and, of course, schools – other aspects of local government have gradually been consolidated into larger and larger units. The creation of unitary authorities in Scotland and Wales was a partial step in this direction. But this is now gathering pace, with proposals to do the same – only bigger – in England and to merge authorities in Scotland and Wales and create seven super-councils in Northern Ireland (from the current 26).

Several functions of local government and other services are also being swallowed up into national or regional agencies. The probation service, which used to have more than 40 local services, has been effectively 'nationalised'. Environmental protection and meat hygiene functions have been aggregated into national agencies. Police forces are likely to be merged into 15 or fewer regional forces, with possibly a single force for the whole of Wales.

And, to be fair to central government, for once they are not doing anything to the rest of the public sector that they are not also doing to themselves.

When New Labour came to power the five largest 'agencies' (or bodies 'working on agency lines') were the prison service, the Benefits Agency, the employment service, Customs & Excise and the Inland Revenue. Since 1997, every one has been the subject of large-scale merger activity and the 'Big Five' have been reduced to the 'Mega Three' (see boxes overleaf).

So what is driving the merger mania? Well, the two overriding themes seem to be efficiency and co-ordination. The Gershon efficiency drive has certainly ramped up the perception that joined-up back-office services, including IT and purchasing, mean big efficiency gains. The 'economies of scale' doctrine is clearly back in fashion in a big way. And this started well before Gershon, as the arguments around the ~~JobcentrePlus~~ Jobcentre Plus merger suggest. But Gershon has certainly given this added momentum.

The second key strand of argument has been around 'joined-up government', especially in the context of providing 'seamless services' to the public. This is closely linked to the idea of focusing on 'outcomes', which fragmented organisations with a narrow focus on single 'outputs' are now seen to have neglected, if not actually damaged.

Notice that ideas such as 'close to the customer' and accountability have disappeared from these arguments. Customer service is still seen as important, but now you don't have to be close to them, just take a customer viewpoint (ie, do some focus groups and surveys and a bit of 'mystery shopping').

Accountability to citizens likewise has retreated into its old, public administration, format – formal accountability through ministers and other elected officials. So, too – for these organisations at least – has the idea that competition is the best route to efficiency gains. Efficiency now comes not from competition and contracts but by 'economies of scale'.

This is not to say that there are no longer elements of decentralisation and fragmentation (and competition) at work. The move to larger but far more independent and competitive NHS foundation trusts is a case of both some consolidation and much more autonomy and competition. The extension of the city academy idea into a wide range of schools is a similar move.

But the reality is that today an individual public servant is much more likely to be working in, or about to be working in, an organisation that is much larger than it was five or ten years ago. Nor is recentralisation restricted to organisational structures. Witness the following statement in this year's Pre-Budget Report (HM Treasury 2005), which formalises the re-centralisation of pay controls into the Treasury: 'Furthermore, to achieve a more co-ordinated approach to pay across the public sector, this Pre-Budget Report announces that the government is establishing a new single gateway for major pay decisions. Reporting to the chief secretary to the Treasury, the gateway will set common objectives for pay across government, extending and strengthening existing arrangements for considering the structure of new pay deals.'

That sounds like centralisation to us. It is not clear how far this trend will go and it would be wrong to extrapolate too much. We will probably not return fully to the old large-scale centralised public bureaucracy model of the 1970s.

Although one of the much-touted benefits of more unbundled and networked systems was supposed to be their ability to be 'nimble' and to react to external challenges and threats more quickly, there are some signs that the default position is 'back to bureaucracy'. After the September 11, 2001 attacks on the US, the reaction of the federal government was not to increase decentralisation, fragmentation and unbundling but precisely the reverse – the Department of Homeland Security is the epitome of 'big is best'.

But it hasn't worked. When Hurricane Katrina hit New Orleans in August it exposed the ineptitude of the Federal Emergency

Management Agency, which had been subsumed into the Homeland Security behemoth. Fema had lost its focus on dealing with natural, as well as terrorist, emergencies and much of its freedom to act independently.

These almost cyclical patterns to reforms – from centralisation to decentralisation and back again – have been noted in some of the management and organisation literature but rarely taken too seriously by either researchers or policy-makers. The reform patterns are never exactly cyclical and things rarely return to their original state. But it does seem that there are irresolvable contradictions – paradoxes – at the heart of public organisations that do produce permanent instability and change.

We seem to be heading back to, if we are not already in, a phase of '(re)bundling government' and 'big is beautiful'. We confidently predict it will not last and that some time – maybe in five years or maybe longer – we'll be back to 'small is beautiful'.

Chapter 17. What goes around comes around

Public Servant 24-02-2006

There is a theory that lurks around the edges of academe and forms part of the folklore of public management - everything moves in cycles.

If we are in favour of decentralisation right now, you can guarantee that centralisation will be back in fashion soon. Small is beautiful is OK, but only for the moment; big is beautiful will be back in favour shortly.

The so-called new public management became the main subject of policy and academic debate in the early 1990s. There are many and various definitions of what it means, but one of the central tenets which nearly everyone agreed with was that big government organisations are bad, breed bureaucracy, create unnecessary delays and complications, fail to focus on clear missions and give managers very little latitude to actually manage.

The cures included decentralisation and disaggregation or, more simply, unbundling government, as we put it in the title of a book Christopher Pollitt and I edited only a couple of years ago (Pollitt and Talbot 2004).

Moves towards decentralisation and breaking up large bureaucracies into smaller, more focused units were widespread. Countries as diverse as Canada, the Netherlands, Jamaica, Latvia and Tanzania adopted and adapted the UKs Next Steps agency model, which was used to break up the civil service into 130 or more executive units.

A couple of months ago, I was asked by the Institute for Public Policy Research to present a paper at a private seminar on the recent merger of the HM Customs & Excise (HMCE) and the Inland Revenue (IR) departments. The new HMRC is a mammoth organisation, at least in UK terms, employing one in five of all civil servants: 100,000 of them in total.

The case of HMRC was fascinating. Back in the early 1990s the two old departments (indeed, two of the oldest in government) were reorganised internally. From a centralised, multifunctional bureaucracy, each was broken down into executive units, with about 30 units in each department.

Although these were internal to HMCE and IR, they were nevertheless now described as working on Next Steps agency lines.

As I already knew, in IR at least this model had been abandoned in around 2000. I found that in fact what had happened was that in both IR and HMCE a process of gradual aggregation of the executive units had taken place during the late 1990s before they had finally been quietly dropped altogether.

The new HMRC makes no pretension to have any agency-like characteristics, which is curious because in the official civil service statistics they are still described as working on agency lines.

So we have an interesting trajectory: centralised, multifunctional bureaucracy (times two); decentralised and partially disaggregated departments (times two); recentralised and re-aggregated departments (times two); centralised department (times one).

This, incidentally, reduces the number of UK civil servants working in agencies from a high point of around 80 % to just over 50 %.

An isolated case, I hear the new public management enthusiasts mutter. Well, not quite. In the past few years the UK has seen a wave of aggregations, with more to come.

The HMRC merger was only undertaken because of the success of the previous merger of two other large agencies Benefits and Employment into Jobcentres Plus. The final one of the big five agencies the Prison Service is in the process of a virtual merger with the newly nationalised Probation Service, which was previously organised in more than 40 local services.

The National Health Service was broken up into NHS Trusts in the early 1990s. There has since a slow process of amalgamations, with the number of trusts shrinking by about 35 %. Proposals to create some super-trusts are in the pipeline.
Local government in England, Scotland, Wales and Northern Ireland is all subject to slightly different pressures to merge into larger units. Police forces are set to shrink from more than 40 to as few as 15 under current proposals. The list is, once you start looking, almost endless and covers most areas of public service.

The new, emerging model if there is a single model is not exactly the same as the old public bureaucracy. There is a strong element of regionalism (large regional structures) in many of the new arrangements. There is also some degree of internal decentralisation, at least in theory, in some of the new proposals; for example in police reorganisation. But that there is a high degree of aggregation, or in most cases re-bundling, is beyond doubt.

This could be just a UK phenomenon but I doubt it. The Volcker Commission on national public service in the US has as its first recommendation: The federal government should be reorganised into a limited number of mission-related executive departments. Sounds a lot like re-bundling government?

Chapter 18. Whitehall shake-up – a premiership starter for No 10

Public Servant 02-10-2006

The arrival of Prime Minister Brown will herald major reorganisation in Whitehall and a massive shift of powers from the Treasury to the Cabinet Office and Number 10, predicts Colin Talbot.

Among all the sound and fury of the Labour leadership crisis the one issue that has tended to take a back seat is the rather boring, but crucial, issue of the "machinery of government". At the heart of Whitehall there lies the Cabinet Office (linked to Number 10) and HM Treasury (linked to Number 11). There has always been tension between these two great centres of power but several interesting things have happened in the nine years since New Labour came to power.

First, they have both become more powerful. There is much talk at the moment about "double devolution" for local government and neighbourhoods, but we have already had a sort of double devolution – only in an upwards direction. More power has been centralised in Whitehall as a whole, as against the 90 % of UK public services that lie outside the civil service. And within Whitehall more power has accrued to both Cabinet Office and Treasury.

Of Whitehall's twin peaks, the Treasury has done rather better than the Cabinet Office. The creation of the spending reviews and associated public service agreements has given the Treasury more power than ever before to interfere in virtually every aspect of policy, but especially domestic policy. The partial merger of the tax and benefits system, the move of national insurance collection to the Inland Revenue, and the merger of the Revenue and Customs departments have given the Treasury ever greater leverage. Having the same Chancellor for nine years has helped too.

Gordon Brown knows better than anyone else just how much power he has accrued and how it can be deployed to frustrate prime ministerial ambitions. A series of Tony Blair's most cherished reforms – especially those involving much greater autonomy to various service delivery organisations such as foundation NHS trusts and academy schools – have become battlegrounds between Cabinet Office and Treasury. To be fair, the Prime Minister and Cabinet Office have fought back. Various aspects of the Cabinet Office and Number 10 have been beefed up with many more policy advisors and units established. There has been talk (yet again) of a Prime Minister's department, which in some ways already exists. But most observers would see the Treasury as having won most overall.

So the question is – what will Brown, assuming it is he, do to the machinery of government when he moves into Number 10? One thing we can be fairly confident of – he is unlikely to leave to his successor in Number 11, however much he trusts him, the full panoply of powers he has accrued since 1997.

This is where the timing of the hand-over of the prime ministerial role becomes so intriguing. Next July, Brown is due to announce the results of his fifth spending review – in this case a "comprehensive" one which will not just set spending for the next three years but set the trend for the next decade. The received wisdom now is that Brown will be in Number 10 before the end of June 2007, leaving the announcement of the spending review to his successor. In some ways this will not matter, as all the main decisions will have been made before the succession takes place. But again, it is unlikely Brown will be comfortable leaving this too much to his successor in the Treasury.

So the likelihood is we will see a massive shift of powers from the Treasury to Number 10 and the Cabinet Office, and probably a reorganisation to create a fully-fledged Prime Minister's Department. Brown has a reputation for hitting the ground running (as with the announcement of independence for the Bank of England) so it is likely we will see this happen within days or weeks of a Brown ascension. And what better way to signal a dynamic new premiership than an historic reorganisation of the centre of Whitehall.

Whitehall Watching

Watch this space...

SECTION 3. PUBLIC SPENDING

I started writing about British Public Spending back in the early days of the New Labour government – partly because I started getting asked by the House of Commons Treasury Select Committee to comment on the new-fangled 'Comprehensive Spending Reviews' and associated 'Public Service Agreements' (see SECTION 3 below for more on these).

Back then – before the 2008 Global Financial Crisis and its massive impact on public finances in the UK – it was a fairly niche subject.

This was partly because the two main political parties – Labour and Conservatives – more or less agreed on the overall package of public spending. It wasn't until after 2008 that the Conservatives suddenly discovered they were "austerity hawks" and that New Labour had been being (according to them) profligate with the public finances for the previous decade. They never have explained how they failed to notice this prior to 2008.

So 2000-2008 was an era of big increases in public spending – especially on health and education – that was largely politically uncontroversial. The New Labour government never strayed far from their self-imposed fiscal rules, which were themselves modelled on the so-called 'Maastricht criteria' for joining the Euro (no more than 3% of GDP annual government deficit and no more than 40% of GDP government debt).

Much of what I wrote at the time was about the new attempts to rationalise the public spending process – the Spending Reviews that started in 1998 - overseen by Gordon Brown. My method was to take the Government at their word and then analyse what they *actually* did against what they *said* they were doing. It almost never failed to throw up some interesting discrepancies.

Chapter 19. The Growing Crisis in Government (Under) Spending

PA Times 28-11-2001

For the first two years of the New Labour government, after 1997, Gordon Brown prided himself on being known as the Iron Chancellor. Public spending was held rigidly to levels set by the outgoing Conservative government, as levels so tight that even the former Tory Chancellor, Ken Clarke, says were probably too low.

In 1998, with the announcement of the first 'Comprehensive Spending Review' (CSR) (HM Treasury 1998), Gordon Brown changed course. Public spending was set to grow again over the three years of the CRS's projections from 1999 to 2002. A second Spending Review in 2000 (HM Treasury 2000) announced further growth projections up until 2004.

The two spending reviews' ratcheting up of public spending were either hailed as a great progress or condemned as profligate excess, depending on political persuasion. What has gone largely un-noticed is that a lot of the proposed new spending simply hasn't happened, and the problem is getting worse.

So where has all the money **not** gone?

In 1999-2000 the government undershot its own final spending targets by £8.2 billion, nearly half of which (£4.5 billion) was in 'Departmental Expenditure Limits' (DEL) – the supposedly relatively stable and planned part of public expenditure under Brown's new regime. By 2000/2001 the DEL under spending had increased to £6.25 billion, in cash terms.

The detailed picture shows where the problems lie. Figure 1 shows that in virtually every major area of public spending – including those covering health, education and transport – there was not only significant under spending but the picture is getting worse, not better.

Figure 1 Under spend (£ billion) on Department Expenditure Limits (DEL)

	1999	2000	Change
Education & Employment	0.83	1.44	0.61
Welfare to Work	0.76	0.39	-0.37
DETR - main programmes	0.53	0.92	0.39
Scotland	0.44	0.65	0.21
Trade & Industry	0.40	0.75	0.35
Defence	0.32	0.07	-0.25
Health	0.18	0.51	0.33
DETR - Local & Reg. Govt	0.02	0.06	0.04
Other	1.01	1.46	0.45
Total	4.49	6.25	1.76

Source: Public Expenditure Provisional Outturn, July 2000 & July 2001

The major culprit of 1999-2000 was the 'Welfare to Work' programme – which undershot its targets by more than 50% (see Figure 2). This was corrected the following year mainly by reducing its budget. But only one Department – Defence – managed to control its under spending. In virtually all other major areas of spending the under-shooting of targets increased.

Figure 2 Under spend as a % final DEL by Department

	1999	2000	Change
Education & Employment	5.2	7.6	2.4
Welfare to Work	50.7	22.8	-27.9
DETR - main programmes	5.1	8.2	3.1
Scotland	3.1	4.2	1.1
Trade & Industry	12.0	19.3	7.3
Defence	1.4	0.3	-1.1
Health	0.4	1.1	0.7

DETR - Local & Reg. Govt	0.1	0.2	0.1
Other	2.7	3.5	0.8
Total	2.5	3.2	0.67

Source: Public Expenditure Provisional Outturn, July 2000 & July 2001

Given Prime Minister Blair's very public commitments to "education, education, education" in the 1997 General Election campaign and to raise health spending to European levels in the 2001 campaign, the fact that both education and health managed to increase their share of rising levels of under spending in 2000/01 must be particularly worrying (see Figure 3).

Figure 3 Underspend as % of total under spend

	1999	2000	Change
Education & Employment	18.4	23.0	4.61
Welfare to Work	17.0	6.2	-10.81
DETR - main programmes	11.8	14.7	2.86
Scotland	9.8	10.4	0.62
Trade & Industry	8.9	12.0	3.09
Defence	7.1	1.2	-5.93
Health	4.0	8.2	4.23
DETR - Local & Reg. Govt	0.5	1.0	0.46
Other	22.5	23.4	0.88
Total	100	100	N/a

Source: Public Expenditure Provisional Outturn, July 2000 & July 2001

Causes

So what is causing this picture to emerge? There is probably no one single 'smoking gun' but a series of factors that combine to frustrate the Government's ambitions. Some of these could have been foreseen, and were by some commentators, and managed whilst others are less tractable.

Labour Markets

The problems of recruitment in teaching and health, especially nursing, have been widely reported. The causes – relatively healthy labour markets, low pay, and low public esteem (in the case of teachers) – have also been widely discussed. These clearly contribute to under spending problems.

Capital Projects

A new study by the Institute of Fiscal Studies entitled "Twenty-Five Years of Falling Investment?" gives clues to the second problem – capital projects. The IFS study emphasises that we have had a very long period of low capital spending. One consequence of this, which I pointed out to the Treasury Select Committee last year, is that in many public organisations the capacity to specify, contract and manage large investment projects has been severely eroded. The fact that the Ministry of Defence (which uniquely amongst government departments has always needed an ongoing capacity for managing large projects) has managed to catch up with its spending plans tends to confirm this view.

The IFS study also points out that the new emphasis on 'public-private partnerships' (PPP) and the private finance initiative (PFI) has a perverse effect – some chunks of what is really 'public' spending is now being carried out by the private sector. The public sector only pays for this on the 'never-never' and so some real expansion in public sector capacity simply doesn't show-up on the books.

Erratic Planning

The new 'Comprehensive Spending Review' process was hailed (by the Government) as a revolution in public spending. The use of three year Department Expenditure Limits (DEL), coupled with increased "end year flexibility" (allowing carry over of budget into the next year) would allow Departmental mandarins and others to carefully plan their spending.
The reality of this supposed rational system has been overcome by the 'usual suspect' in public spending – politics.

The first CSR (1998) covered a fixed set of three-year plans from 1999 to 2002 (HM Treasury 1998). The second SR (2000) covered fixed budgets for three years from 2001 to 2004 (HM Treasury 2000). It doesn't take a genius to notice that CSR 1998 and SR 2000 were two years apart, not three, and that the plans for the last year of CSR 1998 - 2002 – bore little relationship to the plans for the same year contained in SR 2000. In fact they had increased by some £12 billion. Nor was this a 'one off' – Chancellor Brown has altered his overall spending plans for Departments at every budget, and sometimes even in interim announcements, during the past few years. Because these announcements have nearly always been about increased public spending, those managing the budgets have been perhaps not surprisingly silent about the disruption to plans every twist and turn brings. If similar changes in a downward direction had happened it would have been a different story. What is obvious is that it has not helped in planning to meet the new, increased, targets for spending.

Consequences

What are the consequences of this growing problem?

Firstly, public services that should be being delivered are not. £6.25 billion is a very large amount of money that if translated into doctors, nurses, teachers, police officers and the facilities to support them would seriously improve these services. Whilst under spending has a positive side (Gordon Brown has been able to pay back more public debt, and therefore reduce long-term commitments and avoid tax rises) in the current political climate it is pretty clear it is improved 'delivery' that the public wants.

Secondly, the under spending has a less obvious but no less important effect – it corrodes our democratic processes. During the last General Election campaign the Tories were committed to reduce Labour spending by about £8 billion, whilst the Liberal Democrats wanted to increase it by similar amounts. At the time the under spending in Labour's programmes was running at about £8.2 billion, but this was hardly mentioned in the slanging match about whose plans were best.

New Labour's spin machine has been at work. The latest figures on the under spend are carefully hidden on the Treasury's web site – it took me nearly an hour to find them despite the fact that I use it frequently. Figures are manipulated to paint the best picture. The totals for Annually Managed Expenditure in the latest White Paper are compared not with the original CSR 1998 forecasts – which would show a shortfall of £7.2 billion, rather than the £4.5 billion reported against later projections.

None of this makes for a healthy, open debate about public finances. More importantly it does little to address the problem, because the Government doesn't even want to admit it has one.

Chapter 20. It's politics, not planning

Public Finance 23-04-2004

For the Labour government, the amount of investment it has pumped into the public services remains a key vote winner. But the reality behind the political rhetoric is very different. Colin Talbot explains.

Much of the recent debate about public finances in the UK has had a slightly surreal quality about it. Both Chancellor Gordon Brown and his critics would have us believe that he has been throwing money at public services like there was no tomorrow. Unprecedented largesse has been lavished on health, education and other services.

The real problem, we are told, is not spending but delivery. According to the government, it is happening, but we don't really believe it. We may experience better services but believe this is just a spot of personal good luck, while everywhere else they are still crumbling.

The Tories take up the charge that Gordon and Co can spend but not deliver. But the truth behind these flights of rhetoric is somewhat more prosaic: the chancellor has mainly rectified the massive cuts in spending he himself made in the first couple of years of New Labour. Despite his recent spending increases, we are still below the average levels of spending of the Major government.

In July, Brown will announce the outcome of the fourth round of Spending Reviews – SR2004 as it is known in Whitehall. There should be few surprises, although it cannot be ruled out that Brown will try to produce a few headline-grabbing extras as the general election looms nearer.

But the main bones of SR2004 are already known – both the spending totals and many of the main blocks of spending were revealed in the March Budget statement. Public spending is expected to level off at about 42% of gross domestic product, and the chancellor believes there will be no substantial hole in the public finances if growth continues as he predicts.

Public spending in the UK has averaged about 43% of GDP over the past 40 years or so. The high point was reached – not surprisingly – under a Labour government in 1975 when it topped 49.9% of GDP. Its lowest point was – very surprisingly to most people – also under Labour, in this case New Labour, when it shrank to just 37.4% in 1999.

The highest sustained period of public spending in fact took place under Margaret Thatcher. It soared to around 48% a year after she took office in 1979 and stayed at or above this level until 1984. It was 1987 before she managed to force it back below the average public spending over the past four decades.
New Labour's preferred spending levels now appear to be around 42% of GDP and, although Brown is not saying so, this seems to be the new orthodoxy.

This puts the government's plans not only below the four-decade average, but below the average for the Tory governments of 1979–97, which ran at 44%. The chancellor can justifiably point out that high Tory spending in the early 1980s was caused by the massive costs of unemployment and borrowing to pay for it as well as tax cuts.

Today, Brownites will argue, we are spending far less on unemployment and only a fraction of what the Tories spent on interest on public debt. More of Brown's 42% of GDP, they say, is finding its way to actual public services, and this is by and large true. But it is hard to see how public spending at 2% below the average of the past four decades is profligate or potentially damaging the economy.

How does the UK compare internationally? We seem to be steadfastly glued to the middle of the road. Among largish Organisation for Economic Co-operation and Development countries, there is a group of high-spending Scandinavian and northern European countries above us (Sweden, 52% of GDP; Denmark, 49%; France, 48%; Germany, 45%).

There is a group of low-spending 'anglo' countries below us (Australia and the US on 32%; Canada, 37%; New Zealand, 37%). We are above the OECD average of 38%, but below the European Union average of 44.3%.
Economists have struggled for a long time to come up with convincing explanations of the part that public expenditure plays in economic performance: the evidence just does not tell a clear picture. Policies popular over the past two decades in many developed countries for 'rolling back the state', to use the famous Thatcherite dictum, were certainly not based on any incontestable evidence.

Not that it has in reality even happened very much. When this revolution was in full swing in 1985, average OECD public spending stood at 37.8% of GDP, exactly where it is two decades later.

There have been changes – Australia knocked 6% off its spending, Canada 8%, New Zealand a staggering 15%. But at the same time others have grown, some dramatically. The Southeast Asian economies of Japan and Korea added 9% and 7% respectively, bringing them up to 38% and 25%.

The country that cut most from its public expenditure was not associated with the so-called 'new public management' reforms at all – it was Ireland, which at 18% had the biggest fall (from 51% to 33%).

So the UK is not unusual. Our public spending has hovered around the low – 40% of GDP – more or less average for OECD countries – for most of the past four decades.

The only times we have deviated substantially have been due to economic crises (as in the mid-1970s and early 1980s) or because chancellors have radically depressed spending, as first Ken Clarke and then, more ruthlessly, Brown did in the late 1990s.

We are settling back, it seems, to around about the norm for most of the second half of the twentieth century. Nothing too radical there, then. The fact that the argument between the two main parties now seems to hinge on whether we should spend 42%

or 40% of GDP on public services suggests not a lot will change in the foreseeable future either.

Brown's second great claim to fame, other than spending levels, is that he has fundamentally restructured the way public finances are managed.

Some changes, such as the introduction of resource accounting, pre-date New Labour, while others are pure Brown: the whole paraphernalia of Spending Reviews; separating annually managed spending and three-year plans, and of course Public Service Agreements.

Last, but not least are the Golden Rule and the sustainable investment rule. This new system was introduced in 1998, after the scrapping of the old Public Expenditure Survey system that had lasted for almost four decades. Many saw this as revolutionary – and 'revolutionary' was indeed the right word, as it was deeply reminiscent of Soviet-style planning with its five-year plans and production quotas.

The system was designed to force government spending departments into strategic planning. It was meant to make them consider carefully where and how to invest, to plan over longer periods, and to work towards clear strategic delivery goals.
Has it worked? The main evidence that it has not can be summed up in two names: Gershon and Lyons.

The Gershon public services efficiency review (Gershon 2004) and the Lyons review of location (Lyons 2004) both assume that departments are not making the best use of their resources. Gershon apparently detects £20bn-worth of annual savings from headquarter overheads, back-office staff and improved processes.

Leaving aside how realistic this is, how can a strategic planning system be working that misses anything like these levels of potential savings? Similarly, how can accounting for capital investment and resource accounting be working if departments are housing 20,000 jobs in London and the Southeast that could be more cheaply located elsewhere?

The government itself has now – belatedly – admitted that its targeting system was too top-down and unwieldy and left huge gaps and perverse incentives. Documents published alongside the Budget show that of the 206 targets and compliance requirements placed on frontline health bodies, less than 40% bore any relation to the high-level Public Service Agreement targets for health.

For policing, the figure was less than 20%, out of 207 targets. The whole system simply broke down between the top and bottom of the chain.

The National Audit Office flagged these problems three years ago, but it took a hard-hitting, well-researched report from the public administration select committee last year to finally spur the government into a proper review of the system, which still falls short (Public Administration Select Committee 2003).

Both the planning and targeting systems have been most undermined by the government itself. The supposed three-year planning cycle for Spending Reviews quickly became a 'three-year planning cycle reviewed every two years', in Treasury-speak that Sir Humphrey would be proud of.

Brown took to announcing substantial increases in public spending in pre-Budget and Budget statements rather than Spending Reviews, while Tony Blair even announced huge changes to health spending in a television interview not related to any planning cycle at all.

Brown's most recent Budget statement pre-empted most of the main conclusions of the SR2004 (Home Office 2004b), which is not due out until July. The problems with targets come in substantial part from ministries announcing initiatives and targets outside any planning cycle – and more geared to the news cycle. In short, politics has triumphed over planning, as it all too frequently has done in the past.

Because most of these changes have been in an upward direction there has been little complaint from public services. It was only when Brown announced large cuts and job losses in specific departments in the Budget that complaints were heard around

Whitehall that this was 'outside of the system' and why hadn't he at least 'waited until SR2004 in July?'
British public services clearly do need modernising and there is undoubtedly scope for some modest improvements to the planning systems. Yet Brown has probably delivered more spending to frontline services in a more sustained way than any chancellor since the great post-war expansion of the 1950s and 1960s.

A more inclusive, flexible approach from our still over-centralised and over-secretive system might just start turning this modest largesse into real delivery. But the UK is far from being a 'big spender' on public services in either historical or international terms.

The people who really need to get a grip are those who exaggerate shamelessly (for their own reasons) just how much we spend on our public services today as a proportion of our national wealth.

Chapter 21. Curiouser and curiouser

Public Finance 29-07-2005

Gordon Brown might mean what he says, but does he say what he means? The government's Alice in Wonderland approach to its Spending Review timings has a lot more to do with politics than economics.

When are 'firm three-year plans' that 'provide a more stable foundation for managing public services' neither firm nor stable? Answer: when they are organised by the Treasury.

These quotes are taken from the very first Comprehensive Spending Review, published by the government in 1998 (HM Treasury 1998). Last week it used almost identical terms to announce that public service spending totals for 2007 to 2008 – the third year of the current review period – would be adhered to.

So why did the government feel the need to announce that their 'firm' spending plans were still on track? What is going on? To understand, we need to go back to the beginning.

In 1998, Chancellor Gordon Brown conducted the CSR in complete secrecy. This delineated a three-year spending plan. The next Spending Review should have been published in July 2001. Instead, it appeared a full 12 months early.
Year three of the 1998 plan was scrapped. In its place came the first year of a new but equally 'firm' three-year plan for 2001 to 2004.

Why did this happen? The simple if somewhat cynical answer is that no-one had realised that a July 2001 Spending Review announcement would have taken place after the general election, pencilled in for May 2001. Labour's generous new spending plans would have offered little electioneering value after the event. Suddenly, in the Treasury's Alice in Wonderland-speak, 'firm three-year plans' became a 'three-year planning cycle reviewed every two years'.

One other small but significant change in wording: in 1998 we had a 'Comprehensive Spending Review'. Since then they have been relabelled as mere 'Spending Reviews'.

We are promised another CSR in 2007, offering a fundamental zero-based public spending evaluation. It would not be too outlandish to assume that after CSR 2007, the 'Comprehensive' will go out, though the Spending Review will remain.

Any speculation that the most recent shift – emphasising the current plan's 'firm' nature – has anything to do with politics, changes at the top or election cycles is obviously pure cynicism. The next general election will be in 2009 or 2010. The next set of spending plans will be announced in July 2007 and – assuming they then revert to two-year cycles – July 2009. This would allow an election to be held in either autumn 2009 or spring 2010.

Now add this to the news that Brown wants to redefine the economic cycle, which has led critics to question whether or not the chancellor's self-imposed 'golden rule' has been broken.
Forget about the golden rule issue for now – Labour has just been re-elected, and though Brown may squirm a bit over the 'cooking the books' accusation, it is not a big problem for him.

Instead, assume for a moment that the dates shift is genuine, that the cycle really did start a bit earlier. This would mean that the next cycle also starts earlier – giving us an economic up-turn, increased tax revenues and improving public finances in, say, 2008 or 2009.

So, assuming a late handover from Blair to Brown and an economic upswing, when would you want to make the big spending announcements?

One thing you can say about Brown is that he thinks strategically – at least when it comes to politics.

But what was CSR planning originally supposed to do? In part it was to 'provide a more stable foundation for managing public services'. Has it? Well, no – or at any rate, there is little evidence for such a claim.

Government departments might have firm two-year budgets (and now get a third year), but the benefits have rarely been felt by local government and other public service providers.

Remember that Whitehall supplies only about 10% of public services. The rest go through local government, the National Health Service, the police, the fire service and so on.
At this level, research and anecdotal accounts both suggest that frontline service managers are still saddled with the dreaded 'annularity' – not knowing until the start of each year what they are going to get but still having to spend it all in that same 12 months.

In fact, there is evidence that matters have worsened. Because Whitehall departments know what their total budgets are in advance, they can play around with redistributing money as much as they like.

The net result is that managers at the business end are even less certain about how much they will get next year, as priorities and mechanisms change so rapidly at the top.
The fact that Whitehall knows how much it has to play with in 2007 doesn't mean that your local town hall does.

Chapter 22. There's no debate

Public Finance 23-06-2006

The promised summer report on next year's Comprehensive Spending Review has yet to materialise, making it unlikely that MPs will be able to discuss it before the recess. But that's par for the course now.

When senior Treasury officials were asked at the Treasury select committee in March when exactly the government was going to publish the pre-Comprehensive Spending Review report, they answered: 'We and ministers always take Parliament into account.'

This report, due to be published this summer, is meant to set out the context for the 2007 CSR (HM Treasury 2007) as part of a great national debate on the future of public services.
The committee members were concerned that if and when the report finally emerged, it would be in the final few days of the parliamentary session, too close to the summer recess for any scrutiny by select committees.

They were further worried because in all the talk about a 'great national debate', Parliament never got a mention.
If the Treasury mandarins were trying to reassure the committee, the above comment certainly didn't help. It was a wonderfully ambiguous turn of phrase, one Sir Humphrey would have been truly proud of. It could be interpreted as: 'Yes, we take you into account and will ensure it is published in good time for you to fully scrutinise and debate.'

Alternatively, it could mean: 'Yes, we take you into account in making sure it comes out when you can do it the least damage through your irksome enquiries.'

What exactly the summer report was or is going to cover has always been a bit mysterious since the chancellor raised it last

December. Nothing very specific has been set down anywhere but, according to the Financial Times on June 14, it is now called a Fundamental Savings Review (Blitz and Timmins 2006). Crucially, according to the FT story, the FSR is being driven by Downing Street rather than the Treasury and the latter is now trying to scupper the whole idea.

Where Tony Blair sees setting the direction of the next decade's public spending and reform as part of his 'legacy' project, the Brownites apparently see it as unwarranted meddling by someone who's on his way out.

Who knows what the truth is behind all this? It certainly seems very unlikely that anything significant is going to emerge for Parliament to scrutinise. First, a lot of decisions about CSR07 have already been taken. The broad envelope of commitments in health, education and international aid are fairly nailed down, although there is a lot of detail to resolve.

In the 2006 Budget (HM Treasury 2006b), Gordon Brown further announced early CSR settlements covering the Department for Work and Pensions, Revenue & Customs, the Cabinet Office and the Treasury itself. There are still some big areas left, such as criminal justice, transport and the environment.

The Home Office in particular must be deeply worried given its recent poor showing (although it will undoubtedly turn its disasters into an appeal for more funds to put them right).
But we know that CSR07 – covering public spending from 2008 to 2011 – is going be tighter than before and the chancellor is projecting a small fall in public spending as a percentage of gross domestic product, so the pressure is going to be on those services not protected or already settled.

If you want any further evidence that the report – whatever it is – isn't going to say much, then the best indicator was the complete silence about it and the 'great national debate' at the recent 'Twenty-first century public services' conference at which both Blair and Brown spoke. Neither highlighted – or, as far as I can remember, even mentioned – either the summer report or the national debate.

This glitzy, heavily stage-managed event at the QEII centre in London was billed as a major discussion about the future of public services – but a debate it wasn't. A string of ministers and current or past Whitehall policy wonks treated us (us being mostly public service leaders, a few academics and a bus load of foreign visitors) to their vision of the future – but clearly serious engagement in debate wasn't part of the agenda.

The next Spending Review will represent a watershed in British politics – it will cement the post-Thatcher consensus about the broad size and shape of the welfare state in Britain for the next decade. As such, it is a genuine pity that the government's summer report and the national debate seem to be on ice, pending Gordon and Tony sorting their succession planning out.

The fact that Parliament is being effectively excluded from the debate speaks volumes about the contemporary British political and constitutional settlement.

Chapter 23. Open the books?

Public Finance 29-09-2006

Gordon Brown's plans to devolve more executive power offer a real chance of opening up debate over government spending, starting with the Comprehensive Spending Review. But Colin Talbot somehow doubts that this will come to pass.

Gordon Brown signalled in his Labour Party conference speech that he wants much Executive power to be given away, along the same lines as his early decision to give independence to the Bank of England. He said that he wants more done to 'separate the making of public policy from the independent administration of daily business'. This has been linked to the idea of creating an independent board to run the NHS and also to giving more power to local authorities.

So how about opening up the process of setting spending priorities for greater scrutiny and debate? A generous interpretation of the Cabinet-level policy reviews, tentatively announced last week, might be that this is indeed an attempt to create more open government.

Since the Spending Reviews started in 1998, they have presented the government with a golden opportunity to have a genuine national debate about priorities for spending and performance in government activity. At a time of expanding resources they could have been a focus for a sensible discussion, rather than fraught with the more usual defensive 'turf wars' among policy areas vying to avoid cuts.

That opportunity has been lost as we have had four Spending Reviews, each of which was an almost completely secretive process conducted wholly within the Whitehall village. A few outsiders such as the Local Government Association were sometimes allowed a little peek and even the odd comment, but the reviews largely operated like the traditional Budget process, with the chancellor unveiling the results to an unsuspecting and completely unconsulted public.

Sadly, the new policy reviews seem to have less to do with opening up this process than with a faltering attempt to reassert Cabinet authority – and draw back from the abyss after the alleged attempted coup by the chancellor (had someone seen a preview of Spooks?). Four policy areas – economic competitiveness; public services; security and immigration; and foreign policy – are going to be looked at. As a sign of inclusiveness, both Brownite and Blairite ministers will be sitting on the reviews.

This is actually the second attempt to prise the CSR process out of the iron fist of the Treasury. The first came when the prime minister announced that a pre-CSR report would be published this summer to 'set the scene' for the full-scale review next year. After much prevarication the Treasury finally produced a banal and feeble document as late as possible in the parliamentary timetable to ensure that Blair's 'great national debate' did not fly and Parliament was kept out of the picture.

The new attempt to 'force the Treasury to open up the Comprehensive Spending Review and take more account of views from across government', as the *Financial Times* put it, seems to be simultaneously an attempt to paint a 'unity and renewal' picture after the vicious infighting of recent weeks. But it might also be the price Brown has had to pay for that infamous grin as he left Downing Street. Brown was damaged by that and the new policy reviews might reflect his weakened position. There could also be wider implications for the way spending decisions are made and scrutinised.

Back in 1998 the new Spending Reviews and Public Service Agreements (HM Treasury 1998) were supposedly going to alter forever the way government accounted for itself to 'the public and Parliament'. It might have altered how government reports after the event, but it has done little or nothing to improve participation and consultation before the big decisions are taken. Even the post-hoc reporting part has been weak and unenthusiastically received.

Research that Manchester Business School has just completed suggests that Parliament has taken relatively little notice of the results of PSAs (Johnson and Talbot 2007b). Select committee reports have looked at only a small proportion of the available data and then often in a fairly superficial way. The committees covering the Treasury and public administration have made a couple of substantial and sustained attempts to look at performance reporting systems. Some 'departmental' committees have tried to be more systematic, like home affairs. But mostly examination of PSAs has been at best sporadic.

Why is this? Over the summer, Manchester Business School asked select committee MPs and found a generally sceptical attitude. Most did not feel strongly that PSAs were as central to government policy as the government claims or that they had changed government accountability to Parliament. The MPs were also fairly negative about PSA data and didn't believe the public saw them as accurate. Nor did they think the government was encouraging scrutiny. They did say that their committees lacked the resources to do the job properly. The strongest positive response was to the suggestion that the National Audit Office should become much more involved in helping the committees to scrutinise government performance effectively.

It is still not too late for the government to use the select committees to open up a genuine debate on the priorities for CSR07. Select committees could even take the initiative themselves and schedule autumn hearings on the progress of the process and seek evidence from the government and, more importantly, other interested parties.

But the signs are not good. In January next year, the NAO will publish its latest findings on both the PSAs and the Gershon efficiency savings. So far the NAO reports on both have concluded that the data systems on which they are based are at best suspect. If the government really took these things seriously, as opposed to using them as window dressing, it would have put far more effort into securing accurate and impartially verified reporting, and encouraging debate about it. Instead, when its attempt at producing a government-wide annual report was criticised for selectivity and partiality, instead of correcting the faults it simply stopped publishing it.

Let's be clear here – I am not proposing some constitutionally suspect innovation. Ministers would still decide, and it is they who would be held accountable ultimately for their decisions. But, as the government itself never tired of telling all other parts of the public sector, consultation and even limited participation in decision-making are 'good things'.

It might help to shape policies better by subjecting them to external scrutiny before decisions are taken. It might win further support for the decisions when taken, even if the people offering support didn't get everything they wanted. There is plenty of research evidence that people are more willing to go along with decisions if they are consulted first. None of this is guaranteed, but it would surely be worth trying as an alternative to a process locked away in the latte-filled rooms of Whitehall?

Brown has set out his stall to create a more 'devolved' public sector with less executive power. He has even, in one area at least – war – suggested a much stronger role for Parliament. He has talked about ceding more power to local government and to public managers. He has even hinted at a new constitutional settlement based on a more formalised statement of our constitution.

The one thing he hasn't said is that we also need to strengthen scrutiny of the executive – both its political and its administrative arms. As a report this summer from the Institute for Public Policy Research pointed out, our mandarins escape effective parliamentary scrutiny behind the veil of ministerial accountability (Lodge and Rogers 2006). So if Brown really wants to devolve some power, he might cast his sights from the Treasury building across Parliament Square towards the Houses of Parliament.

Chapter 24. Gordon keeps the goal posts moving on public spending

Public Servant 05-12-2006

The Chancellor promised a radically different system of managing public spending. But in the event, politics seemed to get in the way of strategic financial planning, says Colin Talbot.

Back in 2000, the Treasury produced a little discussion paper which summarised the thinking behind the new system of public expenditure decisions introduced in 1998 by Gordon Brown. The spending reviews and associated public service agreements (PSA) were meant to herald a veritable revolution in the way in which the government did its spending business.

The crucial changes were that public spending would be fixed for three years in advance, allowing government departments a chance to really plan strategically. In return, they would be held to account by the Treasury through tight PSAs focused on outcomes. This addressed two of the six lessons spelled out in the Treasury document: the need to plan for the longer term and to judge success not by inputs (spending) but by outcomes (results).

So with Brown about to leave the Treasury, is part of his legacy a radically different system of managing public finances in the UK?

Let's take "plan for the longer term" first. While the new system has introduced more medium-term planning, its success has been very limited and the main culprit for this has been the Chancellor himself.

The first "comprehensive" Spending Review in 1998 (HM Treasury 1998) was supposed to fix public spending in most areas for three years (1999-2002) and, logically, the next spending review should have been in 2001. But it wasn't. Instead it took place in 2000 (HM Treasury 2000) and the new system became, in a wonderfully Sir Humphrey-like bit of sophistry, "a three-year system reviewed every two years". So we have had spending reviews in 1998, 2000, 2002, 2004 and the next one in...2007? The latest one suddenly became a three-year cycle again, and no one is saying exactly why, or what is planned after 2007.

All of this might sound like academic nit-picking if it didn't affect the way that billions of pounds of taxpayers' money is spent. If settled three-year plans were a Good Thing, presumably rather less settled plans are – while not exactly a Bad Thing – at least not quite what was hoped for.

And the rather malleable periods of the spending reviews have been added to by Brown's penchant for announcing major changes to spending plans between spending reviews. First it was the annual budget which became a vehicle for new spending announcements outside the formal spending reviews. In the past couple of years it has escalated to the pre-Budget report (PBR). Last year's PBR was more like a mini-budget than ever before (HM Treasury 2005). This year's, due on 6 December, is also expected to include some fairly major announcements (HM Treasury 2006a).

The only reason there have not been loud cries of protest from public sector leaders about this instability is because public spending has been rising. Now that we are entering a period of rather more restricted largesse, expect more cries of "foul" every time the goalposts are moved again.

So what about judging success by outcomes? The government's PSA targets did eventually, after a rather shaky start, become focused on outcomes. Whitehall, at first sceptical and resistant, gradually came to realise that these weren't so bad after all. Long-term outcome targets could easily be "massaged", blamed on external factors when things went wrong, and anyway, like spending plans, they changed at least every two years. The signs are now that the Treasury has come to realise that outcome focused PSAs are not a very good management tool. It appears it is looking towards changes that will introduce a "dual track" system. Outcome targets will remain, but the real effort will go into a focus on a clear set of output targets tied closely to cost and efficiency measures which will form the basis of a much tighter, integrated financial and performance "contract" with spending departments.

So how do we mark Brown's final report on his attempts to reform the public spending system? There have certainly been improvements but nowhere near the level that government rhetoric would suggest. Politics – events and the desire for headlines – have all too often derailed the aspiration for more strategic planning. It was ever thus.

The real issue now is what will Prime Minister Brown do with the system he created?

Chapter 25. CSR put on ice for Brown premiership

Public Servant 25-04-2007

A tussle is taking place behind the scenes over how far the policy reviews and spending plans will be part of a Blair legacy or feature in a relaunch of New Labour under new management, says Colin Talbot.

As the ascension of Gordon Brown to the premiership comes ever closer and ever more inevitable, so speculation about what his rule will bring gathers pace.

Normally in the build-up to a possible change of government in a general election the civil service has a well-worn set of procedures. Serious policy announcements are stopped, while the civil service turns its attention to preparing briefs for the possible sets of incoming ministers. So far, so simple.
When a change of prime minister has occurred during a government it has usually been sudden and unpredictable and therefore presents no real problem. The machinery of government simply swings behind the new PM and new team of ministers.

Today we are confronted by a unique situation – the political death of a prime minister foretold. No one really knows what to do; not least because the likely successor is playing his cards so close to his chest, and in any case cannot formally be assumed to be the successor.

There are two big areas worth watching: medium-term policy priorities and reform of the machinery of government. Let's deal with the last one. First, Brown has built up the historic power of the Treasury over spending priorities to unparalleled heights. The whole Comprehensive Spending Review (CSR) and associated public service agreements process has enhanced Treasury power. The merging of the tax and benefits system has brought a whole new area of social policy under Treasury control. Brown is unlikely to leave all this in the hands of his successor. He knows just how easy it is for a chancellor to frustrate a prime minister and he has encouraged the Treasury's natural arrogance.

Second, several major ministries are due for reform. Most prominent is the Home Office. John Reid's plan to split it up seems to have been put on hold but something dramatic is likely to happen. Speculation about the future of the Department of Trade and Industry is almost as rife – recently Sir Howard Davies, director of the London School of Economics and former chairman of the Financial Services Authority, called for its abolition.

All of this tends to suggest that Brown's first 100 days will be marked by a massive upheaval in the machinery of government, which could see a dramatic shift of power from the Treasury to Number 10 and the effective dissolution of two of the great departments of state. This will certainly look dramatic, although how much political mileage there is in it is doubtful – by and large the public is not interested in such details.

Much more important politically will be signalling where a Brown premiership will go in policy terms. Here Brown has a difficult balancing act. He could try the "Al Gore strategy" – pretending that the past 10 years had nothing to do with him and never mentioning Tony Blair. It almost worked for Gore – some would say it did but for a bit of ballot-rigging. At the other extreme is stressing the continuity and stability of government, economic successes and a safe pair of hands, combined with some subtle distancing of Brown from the Blair legacy, most probably on the toxic issue of Iraq.

This leaves the policy processes in an interesting balance – the policy reviews initiated by Blair and the CSR under the control of Brown. Officially these are jointly managed and closely coordinated. But there is still a fundamental tension. While the Blair camp is focused on the legacy, the Brown camp prefers to see the scope of a relaunch of New Labour under new management.

A small sign of this tension is the timing of the CSR announcement. At the Treasury Select Committee in January the Chief Secretary, Stephen Timms, let slip that the announcement – due for July – might not happen until as late as October. What Timms did not admit was that this was because Brown has decided the CSR will not be announced until after he is in Number 10. Even on the most optimistic scenario this will not be until the end of June.

So we can be reasonably confident that whatever else Brown's first 100 days will bring it will include the announcement of the CSR, with maybe a few headline catching promises; and a major restructuring of Whitehall. The rest is anyone's guess.

Chapter 26. Darling's big day offers him little room to manoeuvre

Public Servant 08-10-2007

The Pre-Budget Report and Comprehensive Spending Review should offer the new Chancellor huge scope. The trouble is that Gordon Brown got in there first and set tight parameters.

The new Chancellor's first big House of Commons statement is pencilled in for 16 October and this year it will be a mega statement. Not only will he be making the customary autumn Pre-Budget Report (PBR) but he will also be announcing the plans for public spending for 2008/11 in the Comprehensive Spending Review (HM Treasury 2007).

PBRs had already become – under Gordon Brown – something of a mini-budget with often quite big announcements about tax and spending decisions. So, together with the CSR, this ought to offer Alistair Darling a huge canvas to paint on – except that Gordon got there first.

The broad spending envelope for the next three years had already been long set and everyone knows that it is a small drop in spending as a percentage of national wealth (down just under 1 % to just above 41 % of GDP) but a real terms growth (i.e. after inflation). Look out here for some Punch and Judy knockabout between Chancellor Darling and his shadow George Osborne – when the Tories proposed realterms growth but a reduction in public spending as a proportion of national wealth at the last election New Labour denounced their plans as "cuts". However Osborne and the Tories have somewhat spiked their own guns by announcing over the summer that they will accept and stick to the CSR settlement.

Even worse, in their eagerness to seize on the Northern Rock crisis, they started attacking the government over the "mountain of public and private debt". So if they accept the spending plans for the next three years and want government to further reduce public spending it will be interesting to see how they intend to pay for the spending – increasing taxes perhaps?

More likely the Tories will focus their fire not on the amount of public spending planned by the government but more on the "how". Here they have some ammunition to hand – especially on the health service.

The recent King's Fund report by Sir Derek Wanless showing how the £43bn of extra spending on the NHS – a 50 % realterms increase and now up to nearly 10 % of GDP (near the EU average) has not produced the expected results. Partly this is due to nearly half the extra funding being swallowed up by pay and price increases, but the main reason is that productivity actually appears to have fallen within the NHS.

It may well be that after the CSR we will see another round of "we can be more efficient than you" exchanges, as we did with the Gershon (government) (Gershon 2004) and James (Tories) reviews (James 2005) in the run-up to the last general election. Darling is not just circumscribed in general terms by the spending envelope already having been decided – around one third of spending has already been agreed in early settlements for departments such as the Home Office, Work and Pensions, Justice Ministry, HM Revenue and Customs and the Treasury itself.

So the new Chancellor's room for manoeuvre is very small indeed. That will probably not stop him pulling some surprises – Chancellors almost always try and spring something on these big occasions, as a minimum just to keep everyone awake and, at best, wrong foot their opponents and cheer up the troops behind them. There will also undoubtedly be some focus on the manner of Darling's first Commons' set piece. Gordon Brown doesn't have Tony Blair's charismatic oratorical style but he was OK at introducing some humour and springing the occasional verbal surprise.

Darling is by common agreement somewhat more dry than even the previous Chancellor. But perhaps after the turmoil in the financial markets, a soporific Chancellor might not be a bad thing.

Chapter 27. Beam me up, Scottie

Public Finance 22-02-2008

Three-year spending plans that happen every two years; greater accountability promises that actually sideline Parliament – Comprehensive Spending Reviews are looking more like science fiction than a rational tool for public sector planning. Colin Talbot explains.

Here's a question for Chancellor Darling – when will the next Spending Review be? A simple enough question, but one that the Treasury is currently unable to answer and that Darling will probably not answer either in his March 12 Budget statement.

Let us recall. In 1998, the government published its first 'Comprehensive' Spending Review (HM Treasury 1998). This contained 'firm' plans for the next three years' public spending, with greater year-end flexibilities, which would allow government departments to plan more strategically.

In 2000 came the next 'Spending Review' (HM Treasury 2000) – the 'comprehensive' had been dropped and it came only two years, not three, after CSR1998. This was, of course, not related to the fact that if it had been SR2001, it would have been announced in July 2001, after the planned spring 2001 general election. As it was going to include another big increase in public spending, the government wanted to get it in before the election rather than after, when it would do no political good.

So now we had 'three-year spending plans reviewed every two years', that is, until the last one. Somewhere after SR2004 was announced in July 2004 the three-year plans suddenly became just that – three-year plans. This change of course had nothing to do with the date that Tony Blair was going to step down as PM or where a SR2006 would have been in the likely electoral cycle.

The fact that CSR2007 didn't get announced until October, when it was due in July, also had nothing to do with the change in premiership.

So analysts, parliamentarians, public managers and, of course, the great British public are left to speculate whether the next Spending Review will be in July 2009 or July 2010? I'm sure they talk of little else down the Slug & Lettuce on a cold winter's night. But while this probably doesn't excite much interest, even among the London commentariat, it is important for two reasons.

The first is practical – it matters for strategic planning purposes when decisions are going to be taken. If public sector managers are to plan ahead, it would help to know what the spending cycle is going to be.

The second problem, however, is in many ways far more serious. It goes to the heart of problems with not only the New Labour project, but the general malaise of modern British politics (and other advanced democracies). It is the problematic tension between rationality and politics.

The whole 'spending review' project has been deeply rationalist and managerial. It uses arguments about strategic planning, about 'delivery' and 'performance', about the more effective use of resources, that at one level seem unassailable. It fitted into a wider picture being pushed by the early New Labour government of a far more rational – modernised – approach to public services.

This is set to increase because the three main political parties are now locked in an arms race over 'who would manage the public sector best'. This has largely replaced the ideological battles of the 1970s and 1980s over the size and shape of the public domain. While there will still be plenty of political arguments over the details, all three parties agree on the broad shape of the modern social-market state in Britain.

Both the Conservatives and Liberal Democrats have committed themselves to stick to Labour's spending plans for the first couple of years if they were elected and neither plan any radical contraction or expansion of public spending and taxation. So the argument moves from 'how much?' to 'how well?' we spend public money.

This argument becomes more important for another reason. While there might be a broad consensus about how much we should tax and spend, demands and expectations about what ought to be achieved for this spending continue to rise.

Some of these arguments are well rehearsed, the most notable being an ageing population putting bigger demands on pensions, social and health care, linked to the inflation in health-care costs. But expectations are rising as fast as needs. Again, all three main parties are pumping out promises about the quality of services. In fact, it is an interesting question how much expectations of public services are rising 'spontaneously' and how far because of political rhetoric.

All of this puts much greater pressure to produce, in the pithy US phrase, 'more bang for the buck'. But saying it and doing it are proving two very different things.

Take the health service. The government claims to have saved £5.5bn a year through the 'Gershon' efficiency programme but the Office for National Statistics has calculated that NHS productivity has declined by between 2.5% and 2%, depending on whether you factor in quality improvements or not.

The discrepancy is partly explained by a certain amount of fiddling with the efficiency savings figures, but mainly by something more worrying – efficiency savings in some areas might not only have failed to improve overall productivity, they might even have worsened it. The Commons Public Accounts Committee pointed out last year, for example, that the efficiency 'saving' of almost £1bn from faster throughput (earlier discharge) of patients ignored the fact that readmission rates were escalating, with a reasonable assumption that the former might have something to do with the latter.

What this shows is that even rational, managerial improvements in public services are far harder to achieve than most politicians – of all stripes – are usually prepared to admit. Instead they often remind me of Captain Jean-Luc Picard aboard the Enterprise, ordering his number one to 'make it so'. Making it so in complex public services is not, unfortunately, that easy.

Now I don't think anyone (except a few weird anti-rationalist social scientists) would argue that we should not attempt to make the processes of deciding how to spend public money as well-managed, rational, evidence-based, performance-accountable and efficient as possible. But in a democracy these processes have to be both political and managerial/rationalist, and it is on the political side that the present government has performed so badly.

The Spending Reviews – and their associated Public Service Agreements – were supposed to change the way in which government accounted for itself to 'Parliament and the people', as the original CSR1998 documents put it (HM Treasury 1998). But the government has striven not to involve Parliament but to ensure it is restricted to its traditional, weak scrutiny role. While there have been some feeble attempts to open up the Spending Review process, even within Whitehall there are complaints about lack of consultation and involvement with the Treasury.

The government claims to want to improve citizen involvement in both democratic processes and shaping public services. But at the same time it uses the language of 'customers' to assert that all people really want is a decent service, and they don't care how they get it. All the research suggests that this isn't true: people care about public services not just in terms of what they personally can get out of them, but also in terms of issues such as procedural fairness, equity and even their altruistic effect on society as a whole.

For public service reform to really work the government needs to involve people as customers, citizens, users and taxpayers, and not just appeal to their rational self-interest. Julian Le Grand, sometime government adviser and London School of Economics professor, described this duality in people's attitudes as being like 'knights' and 'knaves' and suggested we had to cater for both motives.

One important way to do this is to radically democratise the whole spending and performance process, from Whitehall down to town halls, schools and hospitals. But just as a 'fish rots from the head', this has to start at the top by turning the Spending Review process into a truly open, democratic and consultative engagement with 'Parliament and the public'. Improve the management, sure, but it's the democratic element that really matters most for public services – and incidentally will probably help improve their management too.

SECTION 4. PERFORMANCE AND EFFICIENCY

In 1998 the New Labour government introduced "Public Service Agreements' (PSAs), which were a set of performance targets for all Whitehall departments linked to their new "Comprehensive Spending Reviews'.

Several myths have grown up about these PSAs. The one is that this new "target" culture was an invention of New Labour. It wasn't. The use of performance measurement, league tables and targets had been growing across the UK public sector since the early 1980s and by the mid 1990s embraced nearly all public services. Indeed the previous Tory government had put the capstone on this system with the introduction of "Output and Performance Analysis" reports for all government departments.

The another is that PSAs were an integral part of the Spending Reviews and informed public spending decisions. They weren't and they didn't. They did run in parallel with Spending Reviews but were hardly connected to them at all inside Whitehall and certainly not in Treasury decisions about where the money went.

But PSAs and later the Delivery Unit and "deliverology" were important aspects of New Labour governance even if, like much else, they rarely did exactly "what they said on the packet".

Another string to New Labour's attempts to improve public services was the Efficiency program initiated by the 2004 Gershon review discussed in some earlier articles. This came as the rapid increase in public spending (relative to GDP) begun in 1999 came to an end with the 2004 Spending Review and the emphasis switched to an even stronger emphasis on 'value for money'.

At the time there was a clash of the efficiency reviews, with the Conservatives producing their own version. I had a memorable clash with George Osborne on BBC's *Newsnight* when I rubbished their efforts as derisory. Labour's weren't much better as I explained at the time in some of the articles in this section.

Chapter 28. A false economy

Public Finance 04-06-2004

From time to time, evidence of invisible people and invisible jobs appear on the government's radar screen: when the Census didn't make sense, when cockle-pickers died in Morecambe Bay. But no concerted effort has been made to find out the true extent of the shadow economy, says Colin Talbot.

In the 1993 film, *A Perfect World* (Eastwood 1993), Clint Eastwood plays a Texas Ranger pursuing an escaped convict (played by Kevin Costner) in the 1960s. But for me the real star of this film was a shiny, new, gadget-laden trailer brought into the chase by the FBI. It had wondrous things such as radio phones and faxes and was clearly going to enable the Feds to catch the fugitive. But then all sorts of things go wrong and it finally crashes because it's not really suitable for 'real world' use.

The film is a fine metaphor for 'the best laid plans' going awry when they come into contact with messy reality. Set in the era of Kennedy and the glamour of technology and planning that put men on the moon, it serves as a reminder that things aren't always how we think they are.

Fast forward from the early 1960s and we find a parallel in the way various government policies, designed in the spirit of a 'perfect world' and the FBI's trailer, go wrong. The government designs a bright, shiny new tax (the poll tax) to replace imperfect old rates only to find that millions of citizens protest and, more worryingly, simply 'disappear' off electoral registers. Billions of pounds remain uncollected and billions more are spent on scrapping the new tax and introducing a replacement.

Then a new policy to make absent fathers' contribution to their children's upkeep is embodied in the Child Support Agency. It can easily collect the money because everyone is either paying taxes or collecting benefits, right? Wrong. After nine years of operation the reality is somewhat different. The CSA has collected only £3.2bn – and still has £5.5bn in outstanding debts, of which almost half is 'possibly' or 'probably' uncollectable or has been written off.

A tiny outbreak of foot and mouth disease is detected and the late (but unlamented) Ministry of Agriculture, Fisheries and Food launches a policy of containment through movement restrictions and slaughter of infected and possibly contaminated herds. The disease spreads far faster and wider than Maff predicts, because movements of animals around the UK far exceed its estimates (by a factor of ten). This is in part attributed to 'bed and breakfasting', the practice of shipping herds around to fool Maff inspectors for subsidy payments. The disease itself was almost certainly imported as part of the illegal trade in meat. The cost to the taxpayer is yet more billions of pounds.

More tragically still are the recent deaths of the cockle-pickers in Morecambe Bay and the fruit pickers in the railway crossing disaster. In both cases, illegal migrant workers were involved.

All of these cases have one factor in common – the shadow economy. They have all been partly caused by, or caused an increase in, the shadow sector and in some cases both.

The poll tax encouraged many people – estimates vary but certainly more than a million – to 'disappear' from local government registers. It is reasonable to assume that a number would have concluded that if you can avoid one tax, why not avoid more – such as income tax and National Insurance?

The CSA rapidly found that tracing fathers through the tax and benefits system proved much more difficult than was anticipated. It is probably the case that much of the possibly or probably 'uncollectable' payments relate to people who have already 'disappeared'. But there is also evidence that being chased has encouraged others to disappear.

The two agricultural cases – foot and mouth and illegal migrant workers – have more to do with pre-existing shadow economic activity than with creating it. Just two weeks ago the Commons environment, food and rural affairs select committee concluded that the government was still failing to take the problem of illegal-labour 'gangmasters' seriously and had failed to commission any research on just how big the problem is. (On a positive note, the MPs did congratulate enforcement agencies on better work on the ground, but recognised they were doing this in an information vacuum.)

By definition, unregistered economic activity is very difficult to measure. But a small but significant academic research effort, some of it sponsored by organisations such as the International Monetary Fund and the International Labour Organisation, has been trying to tackle the problems.

The most prominent international expert in the field is Professor Friedrich Schneider of Austria, who has been exploring the subject for years. In his recent book with Dominik Enste, *The shadow economy* (Schneider and Enste 2003), he outlines a number of ways in which reasonable estimates for shadow economic activities can be made. The key message from these is that the informal sector is much bigger than is usually supposed – especially in developed countries.

Dr Michael Samers of Nottingham University has also been involved in field research trying to establish just how big the informal, cash-in-hand sector has become. Again, the message is that it is a lot bigger than policy-makers seem willing to recognise.

Both Samers and Schneider spoke last week at a conference called 'The invisible hand's shadow', organised by Nottingham University's Nottingham Policy Centre. Other speakers covered topics such as taxation, migration, agriculture, child support and the Census. The common theme was that the shadow economy has wide-ranging effects. Some of these are what might be called 'first order' effects: the most obvious is a failure to collect taxes, child support payments and so on. There are also 'second order' effects, where the size and impact of the shadow economy undermine all sorts of other public sector activities.

One thing that is not at all clear is why this is happening. All over the world, the shadow sector has been historically growing, with fluctuations. In some developing and transitional countries, 'state failure' in various forms has been a big factor, but the causes in the developed world seem more difficult to pin down. One of the important messages to come from the conference is that too little research is being conducted.

As the shadow sector grows, national statistics become increasingly unreliable. Just how big the problem is might be gauged from the so-called 'missing million' from the 2001 Census (Office for National Statistics 2001). The results showed that the Office for National Statistics' cumulative estimates since the previous Census – based on carefully designed sample surveys and elaborate statistical models – were out by a million people, most of them (800,000) young working age men. As journalist Graham Bowley pointed out at the conference, the ONS's explanations for this were ad hoc and amazingly flimsy.
So what is the impact of all this on public services? Let us take local government as an example. Local authority income is closely related to information about population, deprivation, local economic activity and so on. If, as seems likely, shadow economic activity is somewhere in the region of 13% of gross national product in the UK (Schneider) – and this is concentrated more in some areas than in others – then some local authorities' incomes are going to be substantially unrelated to the real state of their local economy.

Moreover, much local (and regional) planning activity is based on these figures – planning for homes, roads and other infrastructure. Planning is never easy – how much more difficult when local economic data might be 10% or 20% adrift? Local authorities collect taxes and pay out benefits. That there is a level of fraud and evasion in both is well known, but how well known given these levels of shadow economic activity and of 'disappeared' people?

Town halls also enforce regulations – about environmental health, transport (taxis), planning, etc. How much more difficult does this job become as the shadow sector grows? The massive growth in professionalised 'car boot sales' is a good example of local enforcement by trading standards and environmental health struggling to keep up with sellers of counterfeit goods, illegally imported drinks and cigarettes and home-killed meat.

As the number of shadow workers grows – both domestic and imported – the government is more and more likely to require public services, including local authorities, to check whether applicants for services are entitled to them. This is already causing problems in health, with midwives refusing to co-operate. How long before local government is similarly affected?

Finally, local authorities now contract out large areas of service delivery. How many of the people being paid to provide local services are working 'cash in hand' or using fake papers? Casual labour is pretty common in many of the manual jobs that are contracted out, so the answer is probably quite a few.

It would be easy to repeat the above exercise for regional and national government, the health service and many other parts of the public sector.

How can the shadow sector be combated? The papers at last week's conference started to make some tantalising but inconclusive suggestions. Professor John Hasseldine of Nottingham University Business School has carried out some fascinating work on tax returns. This shows that audit and inspection are the most effective ways of increasing returns – but that persuasion, on citizenship grounds, also produces results (and is a lot cheaper) (Hasseldine 1998).

The reverse can also be true – Dr Carole Johnson, research fellow at the Nottingham Policy Centre, argued that the early policies of the Child Support Agency had probably driven people into the shadow sector, while Dr Lynette Kelly, a research fellow at Warwick University, showed how punitive policies towards failed asylum seekers and illegal migrants were forcing many to disappear into the shadow sector. Drs Mel Evans and Stephen Syrett, both lecturers at Middlesex University, on the other hand, demonstrated that the shadow economy has many positive aspects as well as negative ones, functioning as a kind of safety net in some deprived areas (as has always been the case in developing countries). They stressed, as did others, that some of these positive features need to be harnessed rather than enforced out of existence.

What is most fascinating to me – as a public policy specialist – is just how little this tectonic shift in how citizens relate to the state has impacted on policy makers or policy experts. Yet we tend to cling to the illusions of a 'perfect world' in which we confidently believe we know what is going on. The papers at the conference showed fairly conclusively that we might instead be witnessing the rolling back of the state – loss of state control and knowledge – in ways far more profound than anything Margaret Thatcher achieved in the 1980s. Acres of forest were sacrificed to commenting n Thatcherism's changes while the shadow economy remains largely shadowy. But the effects are all around us, if we are willing to look.

The main point of the conference was that academics and the government need to start looking a lot harder than we have been at the shadow economy and its effects, and the best ways to deal with it. The attendance of representatives from the Cabinet Office, Home Office, Inland Revenue, Customs and Excise and Department for Work and Pensions suggests that at last that may be starting to happen.

Chapter 29. Economical with the numbers

Public Finance 23-07-2004

The more one digs into Sir Peter Gershon's efficiency review (Gershon 2004), the more its figures and strategies do not seem to add up.

Treasury officials stated that the reduction in civil service and other staff would account for 10-15% of the savings, while procurement would produce about a third. A further 40% is attributed to 'non-cashable' improvements in service quality and the like – a further £8.6bn in 'savings'.

The target for staff savings is thus between £2.2bn and £3.2bn – or £25,500 and £38,300 per head – which is much less than the widely reported £5bn figure. But these figures raise more questions than they answer.

The Department for Work and Pensions is losing 40,000 staff from efficiency savings, or 47.5% of all the cuts. So the DWP ought to be saving between £1bn and £1.5bn from staff cuts alone – but its proposed total saving is only £960m. How come? The chancellor's departments (mainly Customs & Excise and Inland Revenue) are due to lose 16,850 staff members, or 20% of the total staff cuts, saving between £430m and £645m – but the total departmental saving is supposed to be only £550m. How curious.

Defence is due to lose 15,000 posts – 17.8% of the total – saving between £383m and £574m of its total figure of £2.83bn. This sounds a bit more plausible.

On the other hand, the Department of Health stands to raise only £18m to £27m from staff cuts, out of a staggering £6.47bn overall savings. Education cuts are set to be £50m to £75m out of £4.35bn. This leaves both with enormous savings to make by other means.

If there is one subject that is guaranteed to send most sane people to sleep, it is procurement, which is even duller and more arcane than accountancy. But it accounts for £7.15bn of the promised savings.

The Office of Government Commerce has realised about £500m a year over the past three years from procurement reforms and is planning to raise this to about £1bn annually over the next three years.

This leaves departments (and local government, schools etc) to find another £6bn-plus per year – a pretty tall order in just three years.

In education, a Procurement Centre of Excellence will start work only in April 2005 and produce £1.5bn savings per year – more than triple the OGC's annual of £500m, and this has been up and running for some time. Given the diffuse structure of education (set to get even more diffuse with more autonomy for schools), it seems a trifle optimistic.

Indeed, the purchasing agenda relies on a degree of centralisation and economies of scale that run completely counter to the autonomy policy for foundation schools and hospitals. Cynics might note that Gordon Brown never used the word 'choice' once in his announcement of the Spending Review. It is tempting to speculate that the centralising/ efficiency agenda emanates from the Treasury, while the autonomy/choice programme comes from Number 10.

The most curious aspect of all is the 40% of the £21bn that is not 'cashable'. This is because Gershon includes in his definition of efficiency things such as the improvement in the quality of teaching.

How will we know if these £8.6bn-worth of changes to quality or quantity of outputs – which have no easy monetary equivalent – are achieved? On this there is, as yet, a deafening silence.

Since 1998, the Office for National Statistics has struggled with the problem of how to measure quantitatively and qualitatively public sector outputs. Initial efforts (especially on health) stirred up controversy because the figures seem to show lots of extra cash creating little increase in productivity.

Sir Tony Atkinson's review of productivity measurements is supposed to come up with a better way of doing it, but its 170-page interim report, published this week, demonstrates just how complicated this is going to be (Atkinson 2004). The final report (Atkinson 2005) is not due until next year. Even then it is likely to take two to three years to bed in a new system and is therefore unlikely to be decisive in gauging if the 40% 'non-cash' efficiency savings target has really been met.

In the meantime, government departments are due to publish efficiency technical notes in the autumn, which will set out how they are going to measure their efficiency gains. An awful lot hangs on these – to be precise 40% of Gershon's £21bn. Unless they come up with a convincing way of showing that £8.6bn really has been saved from non-cash benefits, the whole Gershon exercise will end up looking rather foolish.

But will that matter? Making promises about efficiency cuts and performance is always easy – especially when you know Parliament, public and the media have a limited appetite for following these things through. Perhaps that is what some people are relying on?

Chapter 30. Measure for measure

Public Finance 20-08-2004

Amid all the headlines about public service inefficiencies and job culls, little attention has been paid to one surprising fact: there is no real measure of what the public sector produces. This is what the Atkinson review is trying to do, as Colin Talbot explains

The summer 'silly season' seems to have had one continuing theme this year – how many civil servants can you get rid of?

The Tories have responded to Gordon Brown's Spending Review (HM Treasury 2004) and the Gershon (Gershon 2004) and Lyons (Lyons 2004) reviews with their own James Review (James 2005). The latest victim of this arms race towards so-called efficiency savings has been the Department of Trade and Industry. Labour says it can put it on a mild diet (1,300 jobs fewer), the Tories want to starve it (4,000 jobs) and the Liberal Democrats just want to put it out of its misery.

All of this in the context that public services – note, all public services, not just the Civil Service – can save around £21.5bn a year by 2007/08 through an increase in efficiency.

One report that came out just after the Spending Review, but received little attention (apart from a somewhat intemperate broadside from shadow chancellor Oliver Letwin), was the lengthy interim report from the Atkinson Review (Atkinson 2004).

Sir Tony Atkinson, warden of Nuffield College, has been called in by the Office for National Statistics to try to sort out a particularly thorny problem – how to measure what the public sector produces. The interim report covers mostly principles and methodology, plus a lot of detail on the progress made or not made on specifics. The final report (Atkinson 2005) is due in January next year.

It may come as quite a surprise to many people that we do not know – in economic terms – what the public sector in the UK produces. Given that public spending accounts for around 42% of gross domestic product you would have thought we might have some clue. After all, we know pretty well what the private sector produces, and how do we know what 'gross domestic product' is if one large chunk of that 'product' isn't measured. Surely there must be some mistake here?

The truth is that for many years governments in the UK and internationally have been indulging in a polite (and usually unmentioned) fiction: that the output of public spending is basically the same as the inputs, at least as far as national accounts are concerned. Counting economic activity in the private sector is relatively easy because there are obvious measures of activity all in a single denomination – money. But in the public sector things are much more difficult because most public services – whether they are delivered to individuals (such as health care and education) or are public goods (such as roads and street lights) – are free at the point of delivery.

Even where they are charged for through fees, such as driving licences, the money changing hands has negligible economic significance.

So the little hypocrisy that has been practised is rather simple – let's just assume that public sector outputs are basically the same as public sector inputs, which we can measure in monetary terms because we know how much the public sector spends on wages, purchasing, capital goods, etc. This is what Atkinson's report calls the 'output=input' convention (Atkinson 2004).

Strangely the lack of real measurement of output has not been controversial – it is only when the issue has been addressed that a 'can of worms' seems to have been opened up. Rather like the controversies that have dogged unemployment, crime and even, to some degree, inflation statistics, public sector output and productivity seem destined for a bumpy ride.

Leaving aside the problem that counting inputs is not as easy as it sounds, this rather convenient convention has several drawbacks. First, it assumes that the public sector cannot 'add value' to any of the services or goods that it produces. If what comes out is of equal value to what goes in, there can be no added (or subtracted) value.

Secondly, this in turn distorts national accounts, as the larger the public sector the 'flatter' the overall figures. A country with a small public sector would automatically appear to be growing faster than a country with a large public sector simply because the public bit always 'flatlines'.

Thirdly, it assumes that the public sector never changes its productivity. If what goes in always equals what comes out, there can be no productivity improvements, which is clearly ridiculous.

So is there an alternative? The answer is a qualified 'yes', but it is difficult and is likely to be (initially at least) controversial. The simple solution is that we have to (a) count what the public sector produces and then (b) impute some economic value to these volumes of outputs. Both of these stages are highly problematic.

Counting levels of outputs is not as easy as it sounds. For a start, most public services are quite complex in the range of services they provide. Counting each and every aspect of these services is next to impossible. In fact, we do not do this in the private sector – what we mostly count are carefully selected samples of activity. For example, the inflation figures are calculated from a basket of only about 600 items from the thousands, if not millions, of products on sale.

In some services the strategy has been to select one or two measures that encompass most of what the sector does. So in education the principal measure used is the number of pupils in nursery, primary and secondary education weighted by the cost per pupil for the different sectors. Colleges and universities are excluded for this purpose.

Other areas of public activity are rather more tricky than education, which can capture most of what it does in one measure and only excludes a rather small sub-section of activity (mainly post-school education). Criminal justice is much more difficult. The international classification for 'public order and safety', for example, covers the police, fire services, law courts, prisons, research and 'other' (which includes probation for the UK). Coming up with one or two measures that capture this range of activities is impossible. Another factor is that some of this work – such as crime prevention activity – has no obvious outputs, even though it clearly has value.

The second issue with outputs is that volumes do not reflect quality – a factor that is taken into account in the private sector through the pricing mechanism. So to estimate real output it is important to mitigate absolute volumes (such as pupil numbers) with something that estimates the quality of the education they have received. Since 1998 in the UK this has been done using exam results. These quality measures are difficult. The UK is using constant adjustment (0.25%) based on exam results; Italy uses class sizes; the Netherlands uses movement to the next academic level; Sweden plans to adjust for exam failures; and Australia makes no quality adjustment.

The theory is that once an agreed (and robust) set of public sector output measurements (suitably weighted for cost and quality) has been created, it can be used to calculate public sector productivity changes based upon evidence. This in turn will allow public sector spending levels to be converted into monetary estimates of public sector outputs using time series changes. The alternative, as used in Germany for example, is simply to stipulate an assumed change in public sector productivity and apply that number to changes in public sector output value.

There are several problems with this overall approach – none of which is necessarily fatal but some of which might prove to be. The first is simple – politics. All these sorts of measurements of big numbers are potentially controversial as politicians see the resulting statistics as weapons with which to beat opponents. Even something as seemingly 'set' as the inflation figures have become increasingly contested in certain periods – the inclusion or exclusion of housing, for example. When it comes to public spending, productivity and value, the issues become that much more sensitive. Methodologies that might seem no different – or at any rate no more or less technically rigorous – from their private sector counterparts suddenly become highly contentious. There are those who are quite content with the idea that the public sector does not produce any 'value added', and the opposite. So we should not be surprised when the shadow chancellor attacks Atkinson – the Tories believe it is ridiculous to include measures of quality. There will be much more of this sort of argument.

The second issue is that there are genuine technical difficulties with this whole field – if there were not, someone would have solved it all a long time ago. The biggest single problem is how to measure the unmeasurable, services whose outputs are less tangible, such as crime prevention, or simply too complex to measure, such as diplomacy. True, these take up a relatively small proportion of overall public spending compared with direct services and 'transfers' (pensions, social security, etc) but they are significant enough to make a substantial difference to overall figures. Measurement in these areas is even more vulnerable to political attack because they will, by their very nature, be much less technically defensible.

Both of the above are not helped by the fact that the approach adopted is not as inclusive as it could be. Atkinson has already been criticised for producing an interim report (Atkinson 2004) without first consulting the Statistics Commission – the supposed independent guardian of the veracity and reliability of national statistics. The latter has been asking for this role to be made statutory but the government seems reluctant. For national statistics about public sector outputs and productivity to be useful there needs to be a broad measure of agreement across the political and expert spectrum – something Atkinson seems unlikely to achieve at the moment.

It is also worth mentioning what else Atkinson cannot do as well as what, combined with Gershon and Lyons, it might do.

Atkinson will not – as some people seem to hope – be able to answer the question of whether government is really saving £21.5bn by 2007/08. The reason people are hoping this is because a crucial component of the Gershon savings is supposed to come from 'non-cashable' efficiency gains such as improvements in the productivity of teachers. It is unlikely that Atkinson will be able to do this because its purpose is too broad-brush and long-term – it is mainly about improving national accounts and, while there may be useful spin-offs at more micro-levels, this is not at all certain.

Secondly, Atkinson will not answer any questions at all about the outcomes of public spending – something New Labour has put huge emphasis on. The review is focused purely on the outputs of public services, not outcomes. Measuring the quantity and quality of teaching, or of health treatments, may imply something about possible outcomes but it doesn't tell us anything directly about them.

This brings us to the third and final problem: misdirection. Atkinson could, along with Gershon, Lyons and James, take us back to the 1980s' obsession with cost-cutting and efficiency – at the expense of a sense of 'public value' and evaluations of outcomes and policies. There is nothing wrong with any of these reviews by themselves – if, and only if, a similar amount of effort were being devoted to really finding out 'what works' in achieving policy outcomes.

The government has spent millions on so-called evaluations – most of which have been designed simply to confirm their policies. A couple of years ago the Number 10 Strategy Unit produced a fascinating paper on 'creating public value', which began to develop a much more rounded and balanced approach to assessing public services. Unfortunately, this never seemed to get anywhere. It is a pity we now seem to be in danger of lurching back to the narrow economic focus of the 1980s.

Chapter 31. I don't like Mondays – with Carole Johnson and Jay Wiggan

Public Finance 21-10-2005

Sunday is a day of rest – and dread – if you run a public body. For, come Monday, you know you have to run a gauntlet of inspectors, auditors, MPs and others who all have something to say about your service's performance. Colin Talbot, Carole Johnson and Jay Wiggan take pity.

Imagine, if you will, a fictional head of a fictional prison service somewhere on an island country located, oh, let's say in north-west Europe. He's called Will. For Will, it's going to be the week from hell. As he sits in his garden on a quiet Sunday afternoon, he ponders why he ever took this job.

On Monday, the Commission for Racial Equality is going to issue a report about discrimination and violence against black prisoners. Will has seen the draft and the commission is threatening to use their quasi-judicial powers to issue a 'non-discrimination notice', which is legally binding. This would be a disaster for the service, far worse than the outcome of the Stephen Lawrence inquiry (Macpherson 1999), which found the Met Police 'institutionally racist'.

And that's not his only quasi-judicial headache – an Employment Tribunal just found in favour of a 'whistle-blower' and suggested Will gets his act together on personnel policies too.

On Tuesday morning, Will has a meeting at the Home Office, where officials and the minister are going to give him a hard time over his annual performance targets. The results are actually not too bad, but that won't stop them. And that afternoon he will get an extra dose from the Treasury when he has to discuss his budget. With prison numbers soaring, they have to give him more money – but they always want strings and these days that usually means some sort of commitments about the service's contribution to Home Office 'Public Service Agreement' targets and other performance measures.

And they'll want to know about Will's progress in meeting the 'Gershon' efficiency targets (and so will the Office of Government Commerce, or the Gershon Police as they are fondly known, who are coming to visit next week).

On Wednesday, the Commons' home affairs select committee is holding its annual review of the prison service targets – so at least Will will have 'warmed up' the day before. Last year they berated him for having the wrong targets, but it's officially the minister who sets them, not Will.

On Thursday, it's the unions – the prison officers and the civil service unions both have their own ideas about what prison staff should be doing. These inevitably do not quite match the priorities of the service, or any of the other people who seem to think they have the right to tell Will how it should be performing.

Finally it's Friday, but Will isn't thanking any deity for this end-of-the-week day. The prison inspectorate is issuing its annual report – with yet more recommendations on performance priorities. And in between darting between various media studios to defend the service (again), Will's got to sort out the new 'service delivery agreement' with other criminal justice agencies. Yet more performance measures to be sorted, and if possible meshed with all the others.

And just to round the week off he has two other meetings – one with the lobby groups representing prisoners (the Howard League, Prison Reform Trust, etc) and one with those representing victims (Victim Support, etc) and he knows they are both going to want completely different things from him.

The hypothetical week from hell? Well, maybe, but this scenario is all too familiar to managers across most of the public services. The details change from service to service, but the main external actors are usually – to some degree at least – present.

This is what we call the 'performance regime' for each service – the whole array of outside players who can, quite legitimately, use either formal authority or money or both to tell public services how they ought to be performing.

The range of actors includes central ministries (Treasury, Cabinet Office and Number 10), line ministries, Parliament, judicial and quasi-judicial bodies, audit, inspection and regulatory bodies, professional groups and trade unions, users and their representatives, and partner organisations. They don't all have the same power. They don't all even try, in some cases, to use the power they do have – Parliament has been pretty poor at scrutinising performance. They don't all use their power in the same way or for the same ends. But they all can and do try to 'steer' the performance of public services.

Looking at how the national 'performance regime' has evolved in the UK, the past 20 years has experienced rapid change. In the early 1980s, few in central government were interested in performance. The health ministry was an exception. However, in other areas of public services – local government and local health services – there was a fair amount of activity.

The 'centre' only started to get really involved in the late 1980s, with the launch of 'executive agencies' in the civil service – all of which had to have 'key performance indicators'. Using performance measures became increasingly popular, especially when the 'Citizens' Charter' initiative (remember that?) led to government asking the Audit Commission to set performance measures for local government in the early 1990s. At this stage in the 'centre', only the Cabinet Office was showing any real interest, but the Treasury started to get active from the mid-1990s, and in 1998 it really started to throw its weight about with 'Public Service Agreements'.

The role of the Audit Commission in setting around 200 local government performance measures throughout the 1990s is interesting. In the Republic of Ireland, for example, the 42 measures there were negotiated directly between central and local government – no third party audit body was involved. The commission's role is symbolic of the massive growth in audit, inspection and regulation (standard setting) that took place throughout the 1990s. The public service world became a litany of acronyms for these bodies – Nice, Ofsted, Chi, etc. Some of these were old, well established bodies given new teeth but there were many new ones too.

Other actors have been slower to get involved, and mostly been less influential. Parliament has paid little attention to the deluge of performance reporting from public services bodies from ministries to local schools. Contrast this to the US, where Congress initiated the Government Performance and Results Act, under which federal agencies have to report annually on their performance to congressional committees. Closer to home, the Welsh Assembly has played a much more active role in shaping performance priorities in Wales than Parliament has in London. Some parliamentary committees are waking up to the possibilities of using performance for scrutiny and leverage – the home affairs select committee is really doing an annual report on Home Office performance.

Judicial review has been a small, but growing, area of intervention by the courts into public services. And quasi-judicial bodies such as the Commission for Racial Equality and employment tribunals also have an impact. Even public inquiries occasionally change things – the recommendations from the Bichard Inquiry (post-Soham) are nearly all about performance.
We could go on, but we think you get the picture. There are several questions that immediately spring to mind.

First, is all this performance 'steering' by a range of external bodies 'joined up', or are they all after different, often incompatible, things? The answer is probably more towards the 'chaos' than the 'rational' end of this spectrum, although it varies from service to service. Part of the problem is that although some aspects of some performance regimes have been studied, most have not. So we don't really know and we also don't have systematic comparisons across countries, services and time.

The second, does it matter? Well, seemingly it does. One of the most common complaints from service managers – for example in evidence to the Commons' public administration select committee's inquiry, On Target – was about too much and too fragmented audit and scrutiny of performance. The government itself has partially recognised this in its drive to rationalise audit and inspection bodies. In Wales and Scotland the local and central government auditors have already merged.

But is this the right policy? Because we do not know enough about performance regimes and even less about the way they affect different services, we simply don't know whether more rationalised, joined-up, performance regimes are a good or bad thing. Some theorists – notably in some of the 'new science' areas such as 'complexity theory' – suggest that a bit of chaos might be a good thing in external steering and scrutiny, especially for very complex and hard-to-pin-down services.

Thirdly, how do managers cope? Well, we know some of them cheat – they play off one set of imperatives against others or weigh up which ones really matter. We have heard managers talk about the 'P45 targets' – ie, the ones that you get sacked for failing to meet. Obviously, if there are P45 targets, there are also others you can safely ignore. But cheating and game playing are more reported on than actual. In our experience, most managers make serious efforts to get to grips with these, often contradictory, pressures on them for 'better' performance. Some still ignore it and hope it will go away, but most are trying out various ways of managing it.

Chief among these has probably been the growth of various types of 'balanced scorecards'. The 'scorecard' idea – borrowed for once usefully from the private sector – has been adopted and usually adapted to public services as a way of integrating all these conflicting demands. It is early days but some 'early adopters' say they are getting good results.

Finally, assuming the range of actors in any public services performance regime is likely to remain complex and often contradictory, how can services cope? A useful analogy might be drawn from some management theory about the contradictory and paradoxical pressures all managers experience (public and private). The US academic Bob Quinn developed the idea of 'paradoxical management' to meet just this problem. Most fairly good managers, says Quinn, get along by picking between conflicting pressures and just sticking to satisfying one set of them and ignoring the others. Really excellent managers somehow balance the conflicts and make the right moves, in the right place and the right time to satisfy them. The really appallingly bad managers do the same as the excellent ones – changing their actions all the time – but doing the wrong things, in the wrong places and at the wrong times.

Maybe further research will show that that is what the failing public services tend to do in reaction to complex and contradictory performance regimes, while their successful colleagues get it right.

Chapter 32. Mine's a skinny CPA

Public Finance 02-12-2005

CPAs for Whitehall? Don't make me laugh, says Colin Talbot. Sir Gus O'Donnell's Departmental Capability Reviews for central government are far removed from the rigorous external performance assessments that councils are subjected to Whitehall's spin doctors must have been giggling over their frappachinos.

This was undoubtedly Sir Gus O'Donnell's first media coup since taking over as head of the Civil Service – and quite a coup it was. He managed to convince just about everyone that Whitehall was about to be subjected to a new inspection regime, of the sort visited upon the rest of the public sector for quite some time now.

The headline that predominated was 'CPA for Whitehall' – meaning that the rigorous and widely respected Comprehensive Performance Assessment for local government was now to be applied to the mandarins themselves.

To be fair, there is some improvement here. The usual pattern in the UK is for Whitehall to impose reforms on other parts of the public sector and then wait a reasonable time – say a decade or so – before applying them, cautiously and carefully and usually in a watered down form, to itself.

Local government began being subjected to 'compulsory competitive tendering' back in the early 1980s, but it was a full ten years later before its Whitehall equivalent, 'competing for quality' began operation. Just about everyone in the public sector was subjected to targets and performance indicators from the early 1990s onwards, but it wasn't until 1998 that Public Service Agreements emerged (HM Treasury 1998), which put targets on Whitehall departments. Now the supposed CPA for

Whitehall begins only a few years after the real CPA was applied to local government.
So maybe the process is speeding up. Maybe one day we might even see Whitehall doing something to itself before everyone else.

The background of the emergence of Whitehall's Departmental Capability Reviews is interesting and illustrates the often confusing and usually confused way the 'centre' operates. Until quite recently, there were nine separate units in the Cabinet Office, Treasury and Number 10 that had some hand in performance and delivery policies for Whitehall departments.

In the Treasury there is a 'government financial management' team, which has overall responsibility for formulating spending and performance (PSA) policies. Then there are individual departmental spending teams, who negotiate PSA targets with 'their' departments. And finally there is the Office of Government Commerce, which is charged with implementing the Gershon efficiency drive in Whitehall departments.

In the Cabinet Office there was, until recently: the Prime Minister's Delivery Unit (although, confusingly, this is physically located in the Treasury); the Office of Public Services Reform; the Efficiency Review Team; the Strategy Unit; and the Performance Partnerships Unit. And then, of course, there is the Policy Directorate (and its sub-units) in Number 10.

What comes out of this spaghetti junction of units and offices is hardly joined-up.

We currently have:

- Strategic five-year plans for government departments, which were driven mainly by initiatives coming from the Strategy Unit and Number 10 before the last election
- Public Service Agreements and Spending Plans (three years), which are driven by Treasury spending teams
- 'Gershon' efficiency plans, driven by the OGC and the Treasury

- Performance Partnership Agreements – agreements between the Cabinet secretary and permanent secretaries (or departments and the 'centre', meaning the Treasury, Cabinet Office and Number 10), depending on which document

The latter are the immediate origin of the DCRs. One senior official I talked to admitted that there was very little 'joined up' between these various systems for steering and assessing Whitehall's performance. But it was decided to do at least some joining up and marry the Performance Partnerships Unit and the PPAs with the work of the Delivery Unit. The resulting offspring is the new system so carefully spun as 'CPA for Whitehall'.

So are these CPAs? Well, hardly. Comprehensive Performance Assessments are carried out on local government by the Audit Commission, a statutory, non-departmental public body. Whatever one thinks of the CPA methodology, and it has its critics and has just been substantially revised, no-one doubts the impartiality and relative independence of the Audit Commission. Compare this with 'capability reviews'. Sir Gus O'Donnell claimed in a note to the public administration select committee that 'this will not be Whitehall inspecting itself'.

So who will be doing it? The Prime Minister's Delivery Unit will be establishing and directing the teams that carry out the reviews. True, they will include some external people and draw upon the Audit Commission for advice. But does anyone seriously believe a process organised and managed by something called the Prime Minister's Delivery Unit is really not Whitehall inspecting itself?

We have of course (as always in Whitehall) been here before. A few years back there was the equally celebrated 'peer review' process of government departments by people from other government departments. It, too, was touted as being rigorous and 'independent' and turned out to be neither.

There is also a slight clue in the names of the two processes: one is a comprehensive performance assessment, the other a capability review. Spot the difference? CPA does include an element of forward looking – the so-called 'direction of travel' assessment, but it is mainly about what has actually been achieved. Capability reviews are purely about capacity and assumed future achievement (or not). They say nothing about actual performance.

There has been a sorry history of government reporting on its actual performance. When the civil service 'next steps' agencies started up in the late 1980s, the government began publishing an annual review of their performance. In 1999, the review, despite being produced from the Cabinet Office, gave an excellent and reasonably objective account of agencies' successes and failures and was hailed by ministers as a model report. It never appeared again.

You might also recall the infamous government 'annual report'. This purported to give an account of how well the whole of government was doing. It was received with widespread disbelief and hilarity, as it published unaudited successes and quietly ignored failures. I once put it to Sir Richard (now Lord) Wilson – then head of the civil service – that the annual report was not credible. His response was that they had sorted that problem out – they weren't going to publish it any more.

So it comes as little surprise that the 'capability reviews' don't touch on actual performance – far too sensitive. What then might be the alternatives? What would a real CPA for Whitehall look like?

Well, first, it would have to address capability and actual performance. And the data used would have to carry real credibility, which would mean it would have to be independently audited. At the moment the National Audit Office can audit the systems by which performance data is produced, but not the data itself. That would have to change.

Secondly, for this not to be 'Whitehall inspecting itself', someone else would have to do it. The obvious candidate is the NAO and it is strange that the capability reviews will call for help from the Audit Commission but not from the NAO.

Thirdly, and this is really radical, should there not be a role for Parliament in all of this? It is, after all, the body charged with

scrutinising the executive. An obvious possibility would be hearings of select committees around performance and capability reviews for each department prepared by the NAO. That would be a little more like the pressure that local government is subjected to through the CPA process.
But don't hold your breath.

Chapter 33. Semi-detached savings

Public Finance 24-02-2006

The government needs to put its house in order over how it approaches its much-publicised efficiency drive or it may find that the result is to make the public sector even less effective than it was before.

Is the government achieving its efficiency targets, as set out in Sir Peter Gershon's grand plan (Gershon 2004), which was launched alongside the July 2004 Spending Review (HM Treasury 2004)?

The National Audit Office, in its first report on Gershon (Comptroller and Auditor General 2006), says it's not entirely sure, but the government's claims should be treated as 'provisional' and 'subject to further verification'.

I think they mean that the figures are 'provisional' in the sense that an estate agent's description of a house is 'provisional', and that 'further verification' means 'get the surveyors in, that looks like dry rot to me'.
T
he NAO's doubts about government figures have been widely, and rightly, aired. No baselines, poor information systems, inconsistent counting, not counting costs as well as gains, insufficient audit – the list is almost endless.

If this were a financial audit the NAO would not be signing the government's claimed savings off as a fair and accurate record. But this might not bother the government too much – after all, it is only anoraks like me and political opponents who care about the details.

The NAO's doubts about the programme are rather more audacious. Remember, it is constrained by law not to criticise policy. In describing the whole Gershon programme as 'high-risk', and giving some considerable detail to just how high risk it is, the watchdog has come close to criticising the policy design of the efficiency drive itself.

The programme is highly reliant on just a few departments and projects for huge savings, which inevitably makes it risky. But more importantly, in the absence of proper monitoring there is a real risk, says the NAO, of 'unintended falls in the quality of service delivery'. And it goes on to criticise the programme's management.

All in all, even in the usual diplomatic language of the NAO, this was a pretty damning report. But does it go far enough? I'd suggest not, although I don't blame the NAO for this because of the various constraints it works under.

The NAO's study focuses on the detailed projects that make up the efficiency programme – it chose to study 20, £6bn worth, out of some 300 projects overall.

While this sort of close scrutiny has the advantage of getting down to concrete details, it does raise a rather big question. Would it be possible for these 20 projects, or indeed all 300 projects, to be successful and the public sector to be less efficient than it was to start with?

There are several reasons to think this is possible.

A project-based approach means that it is inevitably partial. Achieving efficiency improvements in one part of a complex system does not inevitably mean increased efficiency for the system as a whole.

A small example suffices: in the mid-1980s, NHS hospitals, under pressure from efficiency targets (nothing's new) decided largely to stop dispensing drugs to patients who were being discharged. The result: instant cost saving for each hospital, and an apparent efficiency gain (same output of patients for less inputs).

But this localised gain proved to be an expensive one for the NHS, because patients still had prescriptions that had to be delivered by the independent pharmacists whose cost structure was far higher than hospitals. The actual outcome was a decline in NHS efficiency (same outputs for greater inputs). This is the 'unintended consequences' law applied to project-based efficiency drives.

And then there is the displacement effect – focusing management attention on one part of a complex system may mean that other areas get neglected, rather like putting in CCTV cameras may simply drive crime elsewhere.

The next problem is another paradox – project-based efficiency gains may actually be 'Hawthorne effects' – that is, they result from the current attention being paid to an area of activity, rather than being a sustainable change. This is well-known in pilot projects, which are often highly successful but prove much less so when 'mainstreamed'.

The only way of knowing if overall efficiency is growing or declining in a public service is to measure it overall. This might seem rather obvious, but it seems to have escaped most of those involved in the Gershon debate.

The problem, of course, is that we do not have reliable information – especially about outputs and the quality changes to outputs – that would enable any such analysis to take place.
Although Sir Tony Atkinson and the Office for National Statistics are trying to move in this direction, it is a painfully slow process. And the figures produced so far – mainly for health, as it so happens – have tended to show a decline in productivity over the past few years.

This rather makes the point that localised savings don't necessarily add up to systemic efficiency gains. Or put another way, just because the estate agent's description of the kitchen as 'fully modernised' is accurate, it doesn't mean the place isn't falling down.

Chapter 34. The value of everything

Public Finance 09-06-2006

Is 'public value' a useful tool for democratising public services – or a load of airy-fairy nonsense? Colin Talbot sets out the case for taking it seriously.

There is a new phrase percolating slowly through the policy and public management community in the UK: public value. It made its debut in about 2001, when the Cabinet Office Strategy Unit latched on to Harvard academic Mark Moore's ideas, set out in his 1995 book, *Creating public value* (Moore 1995). These concepts were adopted and adapted through a series of workshops and seminars and eventually emerged as a Strategy Unit paper (Kelly and Muers 2002), published in 2002 and revised in 2004.

Although the paper was authored by unit staffers, including Geoff Mulgan, the discussions had included the enthusiastic participation of Douglas Alexander, then Cabinet Office minister and one of the rising stars of the New Labour government.

After this initial flurry of activity, things seemed to go quiet for a while – possibly because the Treasury appeared to be at best lukewarm about the ideas. However, over the past couple of years, another round of activity has begun. The BBC used 'public value' ideas in its charter renewal submission and continues to develop the notion as a device for evaluating new services.

The Work Foundation, under Will Hutton, has been running a consortium of public organisations developing the ideas further, including the BBC; Department for Culture, Media and Sport; Home Office; Learning and Skills Development Agency; London Borough of Lewisham; Metropolitan Police; NHS Modernisation Agency; Ofcom; and the Royal Opera House.

The influential think-tank the Institute for Public Policy Research has published a couple of reports using public value ideas. If it is not yet a fashion, it is possibly the start of one. So what is it all about?

In some ways, Moore's ideas can be seen as an attempt to weld together the old concerns for the 'public interest' embedded in traditional public administration with the emphasis on efficiency and responsive delivery in the so-called 'new public management'.

NPM thinking has dominated discussions about public sector reform for more than two decades now, especially in the 'anglo' countries but also in cultures as diverse as Japan and Jamaica. It is based on some fairly narrow ideas from economics – about 'rational choice' and 'principal agent' problems. It assumes that ideas from private sector businesses can be imported willy-nilly into the public sector, and so we got internal markets, performance-related pay and all sorts of contractualisation, among other things.

Public value, as conceived by Moore and others, seeks to inject ideas about trust and legitimacy back into thinking about public services. As my colleague at Manchester, Gerry Stoker, puts it, it is a new way of reconciling the search for efficiency with the requirements of democracy in the public sector.

Moore's particular focus is from the perspective of senior public officials running services, and he uses the language of strategic management. How, he asks, do you demonstrate that your service is delivering value for the money the taxpayer puts into it? He argues that senior public managers have to play an active role in shaping the mandate that their agency is given. This runs counter to some of the old versions of public administration, which see public servants as passive implementers of elected politicians' will. Moore says that, as the people most closely involved in running services, public managers have an obligation, as well as an interest, in making sure they get the best and clearest mandate from politicians.

This view is not uncontroversial. David Walker of the Guardian, for example, recently asked what would happen if a Conservative public manager tried to thwart the will of elected Labour politicians – the classic 'Sir Humphrey' problem. Of course, there is a real danger here. But to pretend that public managers don't try to influence policy is just naïve – Yes, Minister was funny precisely because everyone knew that senior civil servants did just that, but maintained the polite fiction that they didn't.

Moore's suggestion that we get these discussions out into the open seems perfectly sensible, so long as the ultimate decisions are still taken by democratically elected politicians.
Public managers – indeed all public service workers – are a valuable knowledge asset. They know how services run best. Does that mean they should be given free rein to run services, as some current fashionable ideas about 'devolving power to the front line' suggest? No, of course not. But it does mean they should be listened to, and we should think very carefully about where we try to draw the boundaries between 'policy' and 'operations'.

Let's take a recent example. There was a small but significant shift in this boundary in the legislation that merged Customs & Excise and the Inland Revenue. For historic reasons, both Customs and the Revenue had total operational independence and a great deal of control over policy. This was done for the good and proper reason that it stopped elected politicians manipulating detailed tax rules to suit their constituencies – and kept their hands out of the till. The new Revenue & Customs has ceded some of this power over policy to the Treasury, in effect to the chancellor. Whether this turns out to be a robust and safe system remains to be seen. What it illustrates is that the boundary between elected politicians and permanent officials is always shifting and somewhat fuzzy, but also always needs to be carefully patrolled.

The second focus of public value is on the radical notion that what the public values is what it values, not some elite-imposed notion of the 'public interest'. Ultimately, public services will create value only if the public sees that it gets more from contributing taxes than from simply buying what it wants in the market place. But what does 'create value' mean?

As Moore points out, public services do two things: provide services and (hopefully) deliver social outcomes. So when an NHS hospital provides a hip operation, it also aims to deliver a healthy and pain-free patient and ultimately maybe even an active citizen, contributing to society and the economy. So all services have a double aspect – immediate delivery to individuals or communities and eventual outcomes. They have to be seen to be creating value in both ways – in delivering services and in their outcomes.

Secondly, who are they creating value for? Here is where it starts to get a little complicated, because, as they say up north, there's nowt so queer as folk. People are fundamentally contradictory. They are both selfish and altruistic. In public service terms, this means people want services that give them what they, or their family, need, but they also usually want public services to operate in public-spirited, altruistic ways – helping the poor and needy regardless of their ability to pay. We value public services for both things, and it makes it very complicated satisfying such contradictory desires.

But I would add a third dimension to self-interest and public interest: procedural interest. A 2002 book, Happiness and economics (Frey and Stutzer 2002), illustrates this desire with various experimental and survey evidence. Essentially, authors Bruno Frey and Alois Stutzer argue that humans value 'fair play' even when they personally lose. And 'fair play', in a public service context, includes not only fair processes in deciding who gets what, but fair and inclusive processes for deciding public policy in the first place – ie, democracy. With some fascinating data they show that the Swiss cantons that most use referendums achieve higher levels of happiness with public institutions than others.

So public value is a trade-off between self, public and procedural interests. The weight given to each of these aspects varies considerably. For example, we tend to value procedural fairness very highly when it comes to things such as paying taxes, collecting benefits and locking people up. We favour, usually, public-spirited action when it comes to helping the very poor or the very sick or victims of man-made or natural disasters. We place a high value on personal interest when it comes to things such as schools for our children.

None of these balances is, however, fixed and none can ignore the other two completely. In many ways, the recent education debate can be seen in these terms: self-interest (parental choice) versus public interest (no two-tier education system) versus procedural interest (fair selection processes).

Creating public value is a constant process of balancing and rebalancing these trade-offs by finding out what the public actually wants from services. Moreover, this three-way yardstick has to be applied at all levels from what resources we dedicate to services, through to the outputs and outcomes they produce.

This might seem to be a fiendishly complicated process, as indeed it is. But when it doesn't work, it soon becomes apparent. If a public service satisfies individuals but ignores public and procedural interests, taxpayers and voters will soon think twice about supporting it. Those in the government who claim that services can be completely 'customer-driven' would soon find that, if they were, the public would stop wanting to pay for them. But the reverse is also true – if a service is oblivious to the needs of the individuals who use it, they will soon let their dissatisfaction be known – either verbally or often these days through the courts.

To all those who think this is airy-fairy nonsense and what is needed is some hard-headed numbers rather than this subjective stuff, there is a simple question: what happened to Arthur Andersen? One of the 'big five' accounting firms, which lasted almost a century, disappeared virtually overnight when its value in the eyes of the public and markets disintegrated in the wake of the Enron scandal. Subjective? Certainly, but most issues of value are. The Child Support Agency has never recovered from its initial failures and probably never will, because nobody really trusts it. That is why the notion of public value is so… valuable.

Chapter 35. 21st century public services – putting (some) people first

Public Servant 22-6-2006

There is no such thing as a free breakfast and Gordon Brown's price for ours was his announcement of a 2 % pay freeze. How this squared with greater devolution of power in public services no one explained.

The conference held in London a couple of weeks ago with the title 21st Century Public Services: Putting People First, was a strange affair: part rock concert, part chat show, all spin and heavily stage-managed participation. Many big guns and serious thinkers were there – Tony Blair, Gordon Brown, Patricia Hewitt, David Miliband, Sir Gus O'Donnell, Sir Michael Barber, Geoff Mulgan. So were large numbers of public servants, from the UK and abroad.

The stage was occupied mainly by ministers and senior civil servants, while the people who actually manage public services were on the receiving end. When practitioners were allowed on stage it was in a carefully choreographed Q&A with the Prime Minister. No leading public service deliverers were given space to air their often passionate criticisms, which were carefully corralled into table discussions and sanitised feedback.

For Whitehall-watchers there were little bits of "Kremlinology" – the original agenda had not included Gordon Brown, but he suddenly appeared as host of the conference breakfast which metamorphosed into a small speech. "Oops, we forgot Gordon" seemed to be the obvious conclusion. But the most ironic thing was the sheer inconsistency of the messages.

The key theme, from the government and carefully selected speakers, was that what the government wanted to create now was a self-sustaining culture of improvement in public services, with far greater autonomy for public managers. In places there were almost apologetic noises that the centralised command and control style adopted by New Labour was clearly problematic. It was, apparently, necessary as the government tackled long-term problems and allocated massive new investment but now this was in place they could afford to devolve more power and adopt a systems approach.

That did not mean, the Prime Minister and others made clear, any slackening in the pace of change. The usual mantra of globalisation, Chinese competition, technological change and the customary leap to the conclusion that therefore everything the government did was right was trotted out. But while the key theme was permanent revolution linked with power to the customer and managers, there were clearly other messages embedded in the event, starting with breakfast.

From breakfast to the main event: mostly politicians and policy wonks telling service deliverers just how much power was being devolved to them to get on and deliver. Did no-one notice the irony?

There is currently a multi-million pound programme of research into public services, but the only academics wheeled out were uncritical fellow-travellers. I had just come from a conference of 200 leading public sector academics from Europe and the US and you could not have found any with such a bland stance as the one academic speaker dug out for this event.

In these cosy confines you would never have guessed that the Home Office was in meltdown, the tax credits system a shambles and farmers' payments in crisis. Public services are better in many areas but there are still growing problems. This conference was a good example of how not to address them.

Chapter 36. Who's the weakest link now?

Public Finance 04-08-2006

Having been quick to judge the rest of the public sector, Whitehall now faces similar scrutiny. And it hasn't fared well. Colin Talbot looks at the impact of capability reviews and applies his own star rating system.

It's official – Whitehall is mediocre at best and in need of urgent reform at worst.

Despite my own and many others misgivings, the Departmental Capability Reviews turned out to have teeth after all. Perhaps it was the high level of scepticism when they were announced which spurred them to be rather more objective than they might have been otherwise, but whatever the reason, they paint a sorry picture of the first four departments to be scrutinised.

Let's look at the headlines first. I thought it would be fun to do to government departments what they have so long done to others – give them 'star ratings'.

So I went through the reviews, added a scoring system and calculated what star rating should be awarded to each department. A five-star department would have received an average of 4.6 points or above across the ten criteria the reviews used to judge departmental capability. The lowest would be a one-star department (1.5 or less average score).

Using their own definitions, this means a department with:

- 5 stars is 'strong' on average across all ten areas.
- 4 stars is 'well placed' to address any gaps
- 3 stars means overall it needs 'development'
- 2 stars means it needs 'urgent development' and
- 1 star means 'serious concerns'

On this basis the ratings don't look good.

The Department for Education and Skills comes out best, with a three-star rating (average 3.5). Next, the Department for Constitutional Affairs also gets three stars (3.3) and so does the Department for Work and Pensions (3.1). Bottom of the lot is the Home Office, with only two stars (2.4 to be precise). So we have three three-star departments in need of 'development', and one two-star in need of 'urgent development'.

After 20 years or more of 'Whitehall knows best' public management reform in the UK, public service managers across the country won't know whether to laugh out loud or bury their heads in despair.

These results are truly appalling. Not one of the four departments can really be described as 'fit for purpose' on these scores. Anything less than a four- or five-star score means they are clearly not functioning as they should. They all need substantial remedial work at best.

A closer look at the figures and reports highlights the main problem areas. The reviews concentrated on three areas: leadership; strategy and delivery. Incidentally, it is worth wondering why they didn't look at policy capacity, given that it is a large chunk of what departments do.

Of these, strategy fared best, getting an average score of 3.8 points across the four departments, or being on average 'well placed'. This is hardly surprising: since New Labour came to power in 1997 there have been numerous attempts to implement 'strategic' systems in Whitehall, not least the whole Spending Review and Public Service Agreements regime (which we'll come back to later).

On leadership, the departments seem in need of some. All four departments score at best three stars and at worst – the poor old Home Office again – only two stars. As senior civil servants have hardly stopped crowing about the excellence of leadership in Whitehall over recent years, these assessments must have come as a real shock.

But it is in the delivery area – the thing which has been closest to Tony Blair's heart in public management reform – that the departments score worst. Three out of four are rated at only two stars – in need of urgent development action.

The Home Office again, of course, but also Constitutional Affairs and Work and Pensions, are rated as having 'significant weaknesses in capability that require urgent action.'
Moreover, this category is 'not well placed to deliver improvement over the medium term', so there will be no 'quick fixes'. One is left wondering what on earth Whitehall has been doing for the past nine years when the prime minister had delivery so high up his agenda?

The above analysis will probably provoke anguish from various quarters in Whitehall. Well, the rest of the public sector has been subject to this sort of crude analysis for years, so perhaps now they may have some inkling of what it is like.

Because, of course, the above analysis is crude, that is the whole point. It gives us a pointer that some things are clearly going badly wrong in Whitehall, but not much more than that.

The whole methodology on which the DCRs are based is not exactly transparent or, from what has been published, terribly robust. So there may be some justified howls of rage from these departments (privately and discreetly, of course). And of course the results tell us nothing about why these apparent problems are happening – but we will leave the 'blame game' until the end of this piece.

First, let's put the reviews into a wider context.

These were, as the name suggests, reviews of departmental 'capability' – they were forward looking, as both Tony Blair and Cabinet secretary Sir Gus O'Donnell, the head of the civil service, emphasised in the documents. So they do not judge actual departmental performance.

There is an assumption that the ratings were about performance and results – they weren't, they were just about capacity. It is, of course, a reasonable inference that if capacity is low, then performance will also probably be low. But this is the 'dog that didn't bark'. Why, when we have had mountains of data since 1999 onwards (under the Public Service Agreements regime) has the review process not carried out a retrospective analysis of actual performance?

This is even more curious because the DCRs are taking place at the same time as the so-called 'second' Comprehensive Spending Review (CSR07), due for publication next July (HM Treasury 2007).

The CSR in 1998 (HM Treasury 1998) introduced the idea of Public Service Agreements – targets for ministries – and since then there have been further spending reviews in 2000 (HM Treasury 2000), 2002 (HM Treasury 2002) and 2004 (HM Treasury 2004) and PSA targets throughout this period. So why is there no comprehensive analysis of how departments have done against PSAs and other performance measures?

Almost simultaneously with the publication of the first four capability reviews (Capability Reviews Team 2006) (Cabinet Office-led), the Treasury published an interim report on CSR07. This contained no analysis of actual performance against PSAs, just a discussion of how they might be reformed in the future.

So who, if anyone, is to blame for these apparently appalling DCR results? Some will argue that it is actually the whole target system that has undermined leadership and delivery in departments. Others will suggest, perhaps with a bit more justification, that the emphasis on efficiency since the Gershon report (Gershon 2004) has forced Whitehall to take its eye off the delivery ball.

A further refrain will probably be, very quietly in Whitehall but more loudly from some retired civil servants, to blame the politicians. 'Initiativitis', meddling ministers and insufferable special advisers will all be fingered for causing the civil servants to slip from their otherwise Rolls Royce standards.

This may be partially true, but to use a familiar argument which Whitehall frequently deploys – others face the same or similar circumstances, yet achieve excellent results. Local government and the health service are not uniformly excellent, but many of their organisations get consistently high ratings in the various capability and performance audits. They all face targets, efficiency drives, political interference and initiative overload too – but they still manage to do well.

As Whitehall constantly tells the rest of the public sector, if some can do well and others don't, there must be a management problem. The senior civil service must shoulder their share of the blame.

The influential Institute of Public Policy Research think-tank is due to publish what is expected to be a very hard-hitting report on Whitehall shortly (Lodge and Rogers 2006). I have written previously in these pages about the absence of the 'national debate' about the future of public services the government announced it wanted last year.

The combination of the IPPR report with these DCRs may just mean we get a debate, but not the one the government wants – a debate about why Whitehall is so bad at delivery, has such weak leadership and can't even yet do strategy properly. In other words, why we need root-and-branch civil service reform.

The centre of this debate has to be about the fundamental status of the civil service. It is important to recall that the civil service only represents about a tenth of the public service and that within it only about a tenth of civil servants work for the 'Whitehall village' which serves ministers and deals with high-policy issues.

This 1% of public servants in Whitehall effectively drives most of what happens in our highly centralised and highly executive-driven system in the UK. In most other advanced democratic countries, other tiers of government have constitutional rights and much greater autonomy and their legislatures usually play a much more active role in holding the executive – ministers and civil servants – to account.

The Whitehall villagers are not only uniquely powerful because of this centralised, executive-driven system, they are also fairly insulated from the rest of the public services. They may have opened up somewhat in recent years, but this has been much more to the private sector than to the rest of the public domain.

In terms of their social origins, qualifications (unqualified either academically or professionally by international standards), and experience (usually no hands-on delivery experience) our senior civil service remains largely as it was 20, 30 or even 40 years ago.

Is it possible to change the civil service without changing some of the institutional context within which it operates? I doubt it. Unless we radically decentralise towards local government and enhance the democratic role of Parliament the scope for real reform is very limited. But some things could be done.

First, the senior civil service should be made much more actively accountable to Parliament. Why not have select committees hold US-style nomination hearings with prospective permanent secretaries? The quaintly named 'Osmotherly rules' should be changed so that civil servants can be called to give evidence in their own right and not merely as, officially at least, mouthpieces for 'their' minister.

And select committees could be given greater powers to name and shame those responsible for major failures as happens elsewhere in public service, with the expectation that disciplinary action would follow, regardless of where the culprit has moved on to within the service.

Secondly, Parliament's role could be enhanced by increasing the power and scope of select committees, especially by giving them much greater resources.

Thirdly, the role of the National Audit Office could be expanded to support select committees and it could be freed of the restrictions which prevent it from questioning policy decisions, a distinction which is almost impossible to maintain, anyway. It should take over jobs like the DCRs.

Fourthly, it should be made mandatory that anyone appointed to a senior civil service post should normally have had at least several years' experience of managing front-line service delivery in the civil or public services.

Finally, all senior posts should be open to competition – it is probably the case that to get the top jobs, candidates will need to have had some civil service experience, but that is no reason to maintain the artificial barriers which still keep most top jobs closed to outsiders.

Chapter 37. Performance anxiety – with Carole Johnson

Public Finance 12-01-2007

Public Service Agreements were meant to keep track of what departments do with taxpayers' money. The problem is that no-one, least of all MPs, pays them much attention. Colin Talbot and Carole Johnson report on moves to reform a 'scrutiny lite' system.

When the government introduced its flagship modernisation policy of Public Service Agreements in 1998, it was jumping on to a public management reform bandwagon. Governing by performance – and especially by outcomes – had become de rigueur.

It was part of an international fashion. One of the earliest and biggest examples of the approach was the Government Performance and Results Act, passed by the US Congress in 1993. Of course, like all fashions, the reforms have taken on their own local colour, spreading well beyond the usual 'Anglo' suspects – the UK, the US, Canada, Australia and New Zealand – to France, Japan and beyond.

According to David Osborne, the American public management guru who has heavily influenced New Labour thinking, government by outcomes has not been confined to federal government in the US but has swept across local and state authorities too. In the UK, PSAs were seen as a way of reassuring voters that extra government spending would be matched by reform. Chancellor Gordon Brown made it clear at the time that additional funding would be available only to public services that met their targets.

Almost ten years on, this outcome-based approach – and in particular PSAs – is coming under growing criticism. A Treasury consultation on the future of the agreements is doing the rounds in Whitehall. Meanwhile, the Treasury select committee is scrutinising PSAs as part of a wider inquiry into 'emerging issues' for the 2007 Comprehensive Spending Review.

Just before Christmas, a National Audit Office report raised serious issues about the quality of data underpinning the PSA and other target-based regimes (Comptroller and Auditor General 2005). One in five of the data systems used by departments were found to be 'not fit for monitoring progress on the key elements of their PSA targets or... had not been established at all'.

NAO head Sir John Bourn warned: 'Without good data, monitoring against targets becomes highly devalued. If we are to have confidence in the performance reported by government against its key objectives, it is crucial that the data systems used to monitor it are robust.'

The problems with PSAs, though, go even deeper than the quality of their data. Governing by outcomes or performance has two main aims: improving management in government and improving the accountability of government. Most attention has been focused on the first – do the new systems really improve the economy, efficiency and effectiveness of governments? Much less attention has been paid to whether the new systems have improved accountability – especially accountability of the executive branch of government to the legislative branch. In short, is anybody listening to the findings?

This is especially important as in two of the four main 'governing by outcomes' countries (the US and France), the initiative for the new systems came originally from the legislative branch of government. And in the UK the government announced when launching them in 1998 that PSAs were to create 'a fundamental change in the accountability of government to Parliament and the people'.

So has it led to such a transformation? Has Parliament, in particular, adapted to the new PSA system? With four rounds of PSAs behind us (1998, 2000, 2002 and 2004), now is a good time to ask just what has altered in the way Parliament holds the government to account?

Members and officials of parliamentary select committees don't seem convinced that much has changed. A survey by Manchester Business School reveals deep scepticism about PSAs (Johnson and Talbot 2007b). One Labour backbencher said: 'I simply do not believe PSAs have had the slightest impact on public service providers or on users. They appear as a management gimmick of neither use nor ornament, but do cost money better spent on services. Weighing the pig never made it any fatter!'

The survey spent some time looking at how far select committees had actually used the PSA data made available to them. We looked at seven spending department select committees (defence, education, health, home affairs, work and pensions, the former office of the deputy prime minister and environment, food and rural affairs) and at their reports over a three-year period (2002 to 2005) to see how much attention they had paid to PSAs (see box on page 19).

The results certainly do not look like a 'fundamental' shift in accountability. Of 270 PSA targets for which data was available to these committees over the three years, we found that only 47 – less than one in five – were mentioned at all in the committees' annual report. This is despite the fact that Parliament's Liaison Committee, the joint body for all select committees, recommends regular scrutiny of PSAs in its set of 'core tasks' for committees.

The picture was slightly better in other committee outputs – 36 other reports referred to PSAs, out of 156 (23%). But detailed examination showed that more often than not the mention was superficial. One or two committees have produced more substantial reports (for example, home affairs), but overall the picture is one of 'scrutiny lite' when it comes to PSAs.

We also looked at the three committees that have some responsibility for scrutinising PSA policy: Treasury, public accounts and public administration. The latter had conducted a major review of all performance reporting in their On target report in July 2003 (Public Administration Select Committee 2003). The Treasury committee had held hearings covering PSAs each time the new Spending Review and PSAs were published. Interestingly, the Public Accounts Committee, the senior committee for scrutinising the executive, appeared to have done very little at all on PSAs.

Why is this the case, when government supposedly sets such great store by PSAs and Parliament has masses of data available to it? We tried to find out from members of the select committees.

Asked if PSAs really were 'an important instrument of government policy', both MPs and officials seemed equally sceptical, only marginally agreeing that they were. Nor did MPs think PSAs had significantly changed the way government accounted for itself to Parliament.

On the quality of PSA data submitted to Parliament, both MPs and clerks were more or less neutral about whether the information was accessible, understandable, reliable, accurate and 'fit for purpose'. Both thought it was insufficient to judge performance.

An MP on the foreign affairs committee criticised the 'one-size-fits-all' approach to make all PSA targets focus on 'outcomes'. Targets drawn up in terms of inputs/outputs would be more relevant and more useful, one said. Another respondent from the education committee questioned the whole way PSAs were arrived at: 'Why have a target for 50% participation in higher education? The Department for Education and Skills was unable to offer a convincing explanation. Are the targets for achievements at Key Stages Two, Three and Four reasonable or appropriate? It has proved very difficult to have any sort of useful dialogue on these issues with the department.'

MPs, and clerks even more so, thought that PSA data were not widely regarded outside of Parliament as an accurate and fair assessment of government performance. MPs felt that the government had not encouraged active scrutiny by Parliament. The clerks were marginally more positive.

Both groups were critical of their own role, with MPs feeling that they had not been successful in scrutinising PSA data. One MP said: 'PSAs are one tool – but not the only way in which select committees can hold the executive to account.' Although there are exceptions – such as a home affairs select committee report on Home Office targets (Home Affairs Select Committee 2005) – in general our research shows that the level of scrutiny of PSAs by select committees is very low.

Both MPs and clerks thought they should report regularly on PSAs, but were not overly enthusiastic – and were slightly divided over whether committees should focus on specific issues rather than regular scrutiny of PSAs.

One MP said: 'PSAs rarely come up in our select committee evidence sessions with user groups, permanent secretaries and ministers.' Another told us: 'To the best of my recollection PSAs have never been mentioned in the select committee in the whole of the past 12 months.' A third added that PSAs were 'virtually never mentioned in the committees I am on'.

Neither group believed that they had sufficient resources to scrutinise PSAs properly. When asked whether the NAO should provide Parliament with an annual assessment of PSAs, they both supported the idea. One clerk suggested that this would allow committees to 'draw down' information where there is cause for concern. Another emphasised that there have been occasions when PSA targets have affected accountability, such as Estelle Morris's resignation as education secretary after failing to reach literacy and numeracy targets. More frequently though, ministerial and public service performance are measured by other standards.

Overall, the survey results suggest that scepticism about the PSAs themselves, among MPs and officials, is feeding a lack of parliamentary enthusiasm for scrutinising them. No wonder then that little has been done to rectify the situation highlighted by the NAO, where so many of the PSA monitoring systems used across government departments are barely adequate.

The NAO recommends that the Treasury should 'challenge departments' measurement arrangements early in the process of developing new PSA measures and targets', and take other measures to strengthen data systems. However, given the importance that the government attaches to PSAs, it is clear that more far-reaching steps will have to be taken.

The level of scepticism on the part of MPs and officials has not gone unnoticed in the Treasury, and a fundamental rethink of how PSAs are used is under way. It should be embedded into the next round of new, slimmed-down PSA targets due out with the CSR.

There are suggestions of a significant change of approach, away from the so-called 'outcomes' focus towards a much more tightly managed emphasis on outputs and efficiency, with integrated financial and non-financial management systems. Outcomes would not be abandoned, but dealt with through more long-term evaluation and policy reviews, rather than focusing on targets.

Ironically, such changes would come as an unwelcome shock to many spending departments. After initial resistance they have adapted well to PSAs, mainly because the long-term, outcome-focused targets offer huge scope for 'ducking and diving' around issues. The failure of current systems to be linked to finances in any obvious way makes this even more pliable. One senior official in Whitehall told us that the Treasury had concluded deals with several departments for CSR07, months before negotiations about PSA targets had even started. 'It's a funny old contract where you agree the price before you even discuss what you're buying,' as they put it.

If the rumours are true, these contracts might be about to get a lot more hard-edged – and governing by outcomes will become much more about governing by outputs. If they do, it will be interesting to see if Parliament also starts to take PSAs – or son-of-PSAs – more seriously as a tool for holding government to account.

Chapter 38. No value in secrecy

Public Finance 26-01-2007

The Gershon efficiency drive has probably saved billions of pounds. But the government's reluctance to reveal just how this was done might undermine the programme's other aim of regaining public trust.

Just before Christmas, the Treasury select committee held hearings on the Pre-Budget Report. In this, the government claimed it had achieved £13.3bn of efficiency savings under the Gershon efficiency programme.

In evidence to the committee, I pointed out that we seemed to have some sort of inverse law operating with regard to Gershon: the bigger the savings claimed, the less information was made easily available about how the figures were arrived at.

The following day, Treasury officials obligingly made this point for me by refusing to give the committee any details of how the £13.3bn had been arrived at, suggesting instead that the MPs trawl through the individual departmental performance reports for the information.

Just to rub salt into the wound, they did actually publish one of the breakdowns of the data the committee was asking for — in their supplement in *Public Finance*. This was obviously a scoop for *PF*, but not so good for parliamentary accountability.

In an effort to get at the truth, I put in a Freedom of Information request asking to see the Office of Government Commerce reports on the progress of the efficiency programme. No prizes for guessing that this was turned down on 'public interest' grounds.

Twenty years ago, a book appeared in the US entitled *The search for government efficiency — from hubris to helplessness* (Downs and Larkey 1986). This scenario is more like 'from hubris to hide-and-seek'.

The Treasury committee published its report this week (Treasury Committee 2006). It certainly made interesting reading, albeit couched in the niceties of Parliamentary language. Even so, it has highlighted the way the Treasury has been so secretive about the Gershon data.

The purpose behind the efficiency drive was obviously two-fold. First, and most obviously, it was concerned with saving money. The context for this was a rapidly expanded public services sector post-1998 in which there was evidence of inefficiencies creeping into the system, for example, Office for National Statistics estimates of falling productivity in the NHS.
We leave aside the question of why the various 'strategic management' systems put in place by New Labour didn't catch these inefficiencies.

The material problem was simple – the growth in real terms spending was going to come to a halt in 2008/09 and if more resources were to continue to be made available for frontline service delivery, they had to be squeezed out from elsewhere.
Hence the plan to 'save' £21.5bn over three years, the most ambitious efficiency programme ever. In contrast, Margaret Thatcher's early 1980s efficiency programme managed only about £0.6bn identified savings, and only half of these were realised in practice.

The second, and more profound, purpose to Gershon was to create, or recreate, trust in public service provision. The drive for efficiency was not just about saving money, it was about convincing the public that their (slightly higher) taxes were being well spent and not frittered away on perks and waste.
The implied deal was that 'we the government will maintain and even slightly increase the tax burden but you the public will get more, and more efficient, services'.

What is crucial to this second objective is that the public trust that real efficiencies are being made and their money isn't being wasted. This is very close to the 'public value' idea that public services have to be efficient, effective and crucially trusted and legitimate to achieve real success.

This is where the government's secrecy and spin about the efficiency programme becomes so important.

No one I have talked to who analyses these things seriously believes that the government really has made £13.3bn worth of savings. But most of us do agree it has probably achieved the biggest single efficiency drive ever – a quantum level above previous efforts. But the comment I hear most often is 'it's all smoke and mirrors'.

So here is the paradox. The government probably has a huge success story on its hands but by having exaggerated its aims in the first place, over-claimed progress and then tried to avoid any serious scrutiny of the results – by Parliament, the National Audit Office, or anyone else – it has contributed to an atmosphere where no one believes it.

So, ironically, the government might be simultaneously saving substantial amounts of money and decreasing public value by being so secretive and unaccountable about the way it reports this.

Chapter 39. You talkin' to me?

Public Finance 23-02-2007

Whitehall's attempts at consultation leave a lot to be desired. But effective policy-making can only be achieved when there is a genuine process of engagement with all the different parties involved.

The recent fiascos over the government's 'fake' consultations – the road-pricing petition and the nuclear power policy review – have highlighted just how far Whitehall is from being able to carry out even good consultations, never mind anything more participative.

Why does this matter? Well there is the obvious objection that fake consultation has the reverse effect to that intended, by generating cynicism instead of engagement.

But it actually goes much deeper than this. Many of the problems we have to tackle in society today are the so-called 'wicked issues', that is, they represent multifaceted problems that are very difficult to unravel.

The recent spate of gun crime and the UNICEF report on children (UNICEF 2007) both signify deep issues that are extremely complex and defy easy answers.

The traditional solutions of the Left – the state will sort it out – and of the Right – the family/market/civil society will solve it – just will not work. These are 'whole system' problems and can be solved only by involving all the elements of the appropriate systems – something Whitehall is appallingly bad at.

A recent Institute for Public Policy Research seminar on 'A smaller, more strategic, centre' focused on this issue.
The collection of former permanent secretaries, government advisers and commentators (including Sir Michael Lyons, Sir

Michael Bichard and Sir Nick Montagu) was remarkably consensual – the Whitehall model is broke.

Several solutions were on offer: making the 'Whitehall village' much more permeable to the rest of the public service; rebalancing the relationship between centre and locality; and rebalancing the relationship between executive and Parliament. Genuine change probably requires all three.

My contribution to the seminar was to argue that four different types of innovation were needed: policy (at the top); organisational (in directly controlled organisations); services and systems (in the wider public domain, which includes some private and third sector organisations); and finally 'social' (in communities).

This is something the Young Foundation has recently published in an interesting report about social innovation, *Social Silicon Valleys* (Young Foundation 2006).

The traditional Whitehall approach is to see innovation as a transmission belt: from policy-making down through organisations, the system and eventually to social change at the bottom.

So the knee-jerk reaction to young people shooting each other is: toughen up legislation, get the police on the case, gear up the criminal justice system and, as an afterthought, mobilise communities.

There are other ways, which start from the premise that problems such as this can be solved only by genuine engagement of all the parties involved to produce policies that can work and simultaneously mobilise resources that can make them work (even if they are not technically perfect). They are being used – but usually at more local levels. 'Future search conferences', 'community visioning' exercises and 'interactive social media' are being experimented with in both organisational and community/policy settings.

The most astounding example I have come across is the Rocky Flats story. This was a highly contaminated US nuclear weapons facility that had to be shut down and cleaned up.

The facility was so controversial it had been subjected to an FBI raid and government, regulatory, business, trade union, environment, and community groups were at logger-heads over its future.

The contractors hired to do the job managed to turn a government-estimated 70-year, $36bn project into one which took just ten years and cost just $6bn.

How did they accomplish this seeming miracle? It was by applying lessons from a growing body of research and action in participatory organisational, policy and community decision-making.

There are numerous examples of real innovation that manage to engage often seemingly implacable foes in joint efforts to solve problems. In the Rocky Flats case, this included managers, workers, trade unions, environmental and community groups. Rocky Flats is now a wildlife refuge.

Participants at the IPPR seminar agreed that some of this is happening in the UK right now – but only at local levels.

Participation Whitehall-style is merely a perfunctory tick-box exercise. Last year, Tony Blair declared that the government was abandoning top-down driven reform in favour of more self-sustaining system-changes.

There's precious little evidence yet of that.

Chapter 40. Are we being served?

Public Finance 04-05-2007

Personalisation is the latest buzzword in the government's public service policy review. But putting the focus on the customer as user rather than as a taxpayer just sidesteps many of the difficult issues.

Back in the late 1980s I worked for the London Borough of Lambeth, in the days when the 'people's republic' was taking on the Conservative government over rate-capping. The comrades organised rallies, mainly attended by the council's own workforce, in which the slogan was usually 'Lambeth services – well worth defending'.

The trouble was, they weren't. Lambeth's services were generally appalling, despite costing far more than many other boroughs'. Those of us – and there weren't many – who cared about real (as opposed to mythical) services were searching for answers.

They came from an unlikely source (unlikely because most of us were from the Left): a best-selling business book. *In search of excellence* (Peters and Waterman 1982), by two McKinsey alumni, Tom Peters and Robert Waterman, was the first business book to hit the bestseller lists. It had a rather simple message: do what you are supposed to do – 'stick to the knitting'. Do it well and, above all, do it for the people who buy your products or services.

'Close to the customer' was not just about good service, but also about finding out what people actually want, as opposed to what you think they want.

Peters' and Waterman's ideas were picked up by equally unlikely champions, various Left-wing Labour and Liberal councils, and supported by the Institute for Local Government Studies at Birmingham which re-packaged *In search of excellence* into what they called the new 'public service orientation' (Clarke and Stewart 1985b) (Some of us tried – and failed – to introduce these ideas into Lambeth, but that's another story).

Now – fast forward 20 years and the Labour government, ten years into office, publishes a much-heralded policy document, *Building on progress: public services* (Prime Minister's Strategy Unit 2007). Launched at another fancy conference on 'Twenty-first century public services' at the QEII Centre in London, the document has one central theme – personalisation of public services. Sounds familiar? Well, yes and no.

The public service orientation was actually twin-themed – it emphasised customer service, yes, but also the democratic role, of local government especially.

Today's Labour policy-makers have ditched the second theme – just as the new personalisation of public services mantra was being lauded in the QEII, Sir Michael Lyons' attempt to revitalise local democracy was being quietly buried by ministers.

So we are left with personalisation as the key theme for public services for the twenty-first century. But what does it mean and can, or indeed should, work?

The main argument for it is simple: people get personalisation in the private sector and now they want – may demand – it in the public domain. Manufacturing and services have become responsive and personal and public services will have to follow suit.

The problem with this argument is also simple: it isn't true. First, some services have undoubtedly become more personalised in the private sector but usually only if the costs of personalisation are small or if you pay for the privilege.

Anyone strolling along our increasingly homogenised high streets for a bit of retail therapy knows only too well just how lacking in personalisation some services are. Take a simple cup of coffee – yes, you can get a highly personalised cup in

Starbucks but it will cost you several times as much as a depersonalised McDonald's brew.

Few people – least of all me – will deny that public services are often too impersonal. They could certainly be better – but the real questions are how much better, and who decides?

As Mark Moore, the Harvard academic and creator of the 'public value' movement, recently pointed out at CIPFA in Scotland's annual conference in Glasgow, you can bet that if public services reached oak-panelled, leather-seating, personal-shopper and latté levels of provision, the customers would soon be up in arms – about having to pay too much tax. And, I would add that if they became too personalised, as in 'personalised' taxation or 'personalised' fines, they would also become rather unpopular.

The truth is that public services will always be a balancing act between the customer-as-taxpayer/citizen and the customer-as-user/participant. New Labour seems to be obsessed with only one aspect of this balancing act – the customer-as-user.

They might be right that we need to 'bend the stick' in the direction of better services to users, including some personalisation – but it is not a costless option. It takes resources, and there is the potential danger of undermining people's commitment to the more collective and, dare I say redistributive, aspects of the public domain.

As with so many other aspects of policy, simplistic rhetoric always seems more attractive to politicians than the complex realities of balancing conflicting interests and contradictory imperatives.

So what's new?

Chapter 41. Skills for government?

Public Finance 10-09-2007

Whitehall is broke and badly needs fixing according to MPs' innocent-sounding Skills for Government report (Public Administration Select Committee 2007b). Leadership is failing the civil service. The government's drive on 'delivery' has yet to revive performance in major departments.

One of the many reports rushed out by parliamentary committees just before the start of the recess was the innocent sounding Skills for Government published by the Public Administration Select Committee (PASC) (Public Administration Select Committee 2007b). In the welter of more sexy reports, this one passed almost unnoticed by the media and yet it was probably the most important one of the lot – because without addressing the issues it raises that none of the other proposed policy changes are likely to succeed in the way they should. Because what PASC says is rather simple – Whitehall is broke and badly needs fixing.

We are familiar with the grim headlines – the Rural Payments Agency's failure to make payments; the Child Support Agency's failure to support children; tax credits' over/under payments; the junior doctors' recruitment fiasco; and the various IT failures. Not everything is broke and some parts of the system still perform tolerably, and in some cases remarkably well, but what this report highlights is not one-off failings but a systemic shortfall in performance.

Based on the government's own Departmental Capability Reviews (DCRs) – 15 of which had been published as of June 2007 – the committee concludes that they "paint a bleak picture of civil service performance" suggesting poor leadership and service delivery and only moderately good strategy-making. Scoring the departments overall, based on the DCRs, the committee gave them only 49 points out of hundred for strategy, 32 for leadership and a miserable 24 for delivery.

The effect on morale is obvious – less than half of civil servants believe their top team provides effective leadership and over a third have little or no confidence in them.

The score for delivery is especially important, given the immense energy which the former Prime Minister Tony Blair put into "delivery, delivery, delivery" as shown in Michael Barber's recent book about the work of the Delivery Unit (Instruction to Deliver).

Indeed Barber asserts that "the failure to grasp the need for radical reform of the civil service in the first term (of New Labour in government) was a mistake which Blair himself came to realise had cost him dearly" (p45) and led directly to setting up the Delivery Unit.

Despite Barber's claims about the successes of his unit, the results of the DCRs suggest the situation hasn't really improved across Whitehall. It could be argued that the Delivery Unit focused on only four departments for most of its work. But according to the PASC report (ibid), these four departments didn't do especially well either – Transport and Education score only 4 out of 10, Health scores 2 and the Home Office a miserable 0. So whilst the Delivery Unit may have produced some improvements in frontline services it seems to have left little impact on the Whitehall machinery, something which Barber and Blair expressly set out to do.

The original reason for the PASC to work on this report (ibid) was the recently initiated Professional Skills for Government programme, which is supposed to remedy some of these ills. PASC is sceptical about whether PSG is anywhere sufficiently radical enough to achieve its objectives.

They are critical of the National School of Government for having "demand-led" strategy, given that Whitehall departments do not have adequate strategies of their own to improve capability and therefore are unlikely to call on the NSG for the right support.

They also point out that whilst the capability reviews have been credible this time because they have been critical, the fact that they are in effect Whitehall scrutinising itself will undermine future reviews that allege improvements in performance. They suggest instead that DCRs need to be independently managed.

They make several recommendations to improve the situation – these include more interchange with the rest of the public sector; better performance management of individuals; better external recruitment – especially at lower levels; better accreditation of skills.

But perhaps their most intriguing suggestion is the creation of a National Performance Office – similar to the National Audit Office – that would scrutinise civil service performance on more than a financial basis, including managing the capability reviews. This seems to me right in principle but wrong in detail. The NAO has a long track record of looking at performance – from its early reports on executive agencies in the early '90s through to government departments and public service agreements since 1997.

It would make more sense to give this role to an expanded NAO but with this remit linked to the PASC and other departmental select committees. The NAO is already expanding its role to support other parliamentary committees than its parent one, the Public Accounts Committee. And there are plenty of international precedents – such as the General Accountability Office in the USA.

What PASC does not point out is that external scrutiny seems to have been a crucial component in public service delivery improvements where they have occurred – Ofsted for education and Comprehensive Performance Assessments for local government being two good examples. If Whitehall is ever going to get its act together, it needs an external watchdog with teeth, firmly linked to parliamentary scrutiny, biting at its heels.

Chapter 42. Slimming down the targets

Public Finance 17-08-2007

The scaling down of Public Service Agreements has been heralded as emblematic of a less centralist approach to performance management. But details of the new delivery agreements suggest otherwise.

One of the constant criticisms of New Labour has been its supposed obsession with targets. This has often been likened to Soviet-style command and control planning, with Gordon Brown accused of having Stalinist tendencies by a former senior official.

To be fair to New Labour, it didn't invent targets. By the time it came to power in 1997 most of the UK public sector had some form of mandated performance reporting: there were already national targets in health, for example.

True, these were not always explicit, but many were and almost no part of the system escaped some form of measurement.
There was one glaring exception – Whitehall itself. Government, or rather ministries, gave themselves no targets. Public Service Agreements –introduced with the Comprehensive Spending Review of 1998 (HM Treasury 1998) – were the pinnacle of this measurement mountain.

From 1998 onwards, government departments had to set targets and report publicly on them. These were then supposed to form the basis of setting targets lower down the system, so 'joining-up' performance drivers from top to bottom.

For the past couple of years the government has been saying that it wants to move towards a more decentralised system. A top-down approach was necessary, so the argument goes, in the early days because public services were failing so badly.
You don't have the luxury of debate and consultation when the house is on fire, you need someone in charge. Failing schools

and long waiting lists for health treatments were crises that had to be dealt with through the smack of firm government.

Now, apparently, the crisis is over: targets worked and the public services are on a more even keel. Now it is time for a more gentle, caring, involving and decentralised approach. Targets are to be mercilessly scythed down and the responsibility for delivering devolved nearer the front line. There is talk of creating 'self-improving systems' that do not require central intervention once established.

Most emblematically, the government is due to announce in October that PSAs – the pinnacle of targetry – are to be vastly scaled down. Andy Burnham, the new chief secretary to the Treasury, announced as much a few weeks ago, in an interview with the Guardian. The subtext here was obvious. The message that targets are dead was itself carefully targeted by announcing it on the front page.

There are two problems with this narrative: money and reality. When the former chief secretary Stephen Timms gave evidence to the Treasury select committee in January he specifically attributed the improvements in health and education to PSAs. But is this really true?

Any sober evaluation of PSAs' impact would have to see them in the context of increased public spending. Are improvements in services a result of PSAs or more money? The answer is probably mixed: in some areas PSAs helped to concentrate the extra resources on priorities in a positive way and in others they were less successful.

The second problem is the reality (as opposed to the spin) about how the new system is supposed to work. PSAs are expected to number about 30 (down from about 160) and will not be tied to individual departments. There will be cross-government priorities, with one department designated as the lead, but with others in the frame in most cases.

The clear implication is that this reduction in top-level targets will be cascaded down into every aspect of public services.

But the detail says otherwise. Underneath each PSA will be a 'delivery agreement'. This will involve all the key players in the 'delivery chain' for this specific target in signing up to their own targets and priorities and monitoring systems to ensure delivery.

If we take an area such as child poverty, this would potentially involve hundreds of central and local public service bodies across multiple Whitehall turfs.

We don't know exactly what will be in these delivery agreements and the Treasury is being as secretive as ever about them.

A cynic might conclude that PSAs were being reduced through the device of pushing the actual target-setting down one level into the delivery agreements and hoping that no-one notices.

So when the Comprehensive Spending Review is published in October, don't just look at the top-level PSAs; look at what's behind them. Then we'll be able to tell if the government really is on a targets diet, or just hiding the chocolate biscuits somewhere else.

Chapter 43. The efficiency of falling productivity

Public Servant 04-03-2008
Conflicting evidence of government efficiencies presents a puzzle even to the government. Colin Talbot, who chairs Public Service Events' Efficiency Challenge conference in London today, looks for some answers.

By June 2007 the government claimed that the Department of Health in England was saving £5.5bn pounds a year in efficiency savings, in a report issued alongside the Comprehensive Spending Review in October 2007 (HM Treasury 2007). That represents just between 6 or 7 % of the Department of Health's spending, depending on which financial year the £5.5bn figure applies to.

In January 2008 the Office for National Statistics issued a report saying that health service productivity has fallen – between 2001 and 2005 it fell between 2.0 and 2.5 % a year, depending on whether you allow for improvements in quality (the 2.0 % figure) or not (the 2.5 %) (Lee 2008).

Confused? You should be. How on earth can the health service be simultaneously saving billions in efficiency savings while its' productivity is declining?

The standard argument being deployed by Department of Health and Treasury officials is that measuring efficiency and productivity are two different things, and anyway the Office of National Statistics is wrong.

First, is the ONS wrong? As far as I can tell the Treasury line seems to be that the ONS measures inputs – the costs of services – wrongly and this leads to an erroneous measurement of productivity. This is laughable – the ONS uses standard, internationally recognised procedures and its analysis is backed by independent research by the Kings Fund.

Moreover everyone knows more or less why the NHS's productivity should have been expected to fall – the very expensive consultants and GPs contracts; the massive influx of new – and inevitably less experienced – staff; the disruptions caused by multiple reorganisations; big building programmes (which inevitably disrupt services in the short term); and so on.

Some of these problems are short term, others are more potentially long term and structural and therefore worrying. But they are all pretty obvious – except to the government, which wants to claim "success" in its extra spending, and of course to its Treasury minions.

The real issue is how can the government claim to be making £5.5bn of efficiency savings in a system whose productivity is falling? There are several possible answers, but I'll mention just two.

The first is what in Whitehall is fondly known as "smoke and mirrors". My most memorable encounter with this phrase was in the mid-1990s when a senior mandarin asked me how his department could make it look like they had cut 25 % of top management posts without actually doing it. "We know it's all smoke and mirrors," he said, and politely asked: "We just wondered if you knew which smoke and which mirrors we should use this time."

Some of them are clearly still at it. Last year the respected Public Accounts Committee reported that the Department of Health, among others, had been using just a touch of smoke and mirrors in their reporting of efficiency savings – manipulating baselines to produce higher apparent savings than otherwise, for example.

But despite these sometimes pretty crude attempts at fiddling, most independent analysis – including my own – suggests that there have been real and substantial efficiency savings, maybe just not as much as the government claims.

The second explanation for the discrepancy between efficiency gains and productivity decline is in many ways more worrying than a bit of game-playing. The problem is one of "levels or units of analysis". The ONS has been trying to measure the overall productivity of an entire system, whereas efficiency measures have concentrated on specific sub-systems.

This is problematic in several ways. First, it is logically possible for local efficiency savings to be made while the global productivity of the system declines. Taking purchasing as an example – let's say real savings are made by buying the same quantity and quality of necessary inputs. This is a genuine efficiency saving.

But suppose the way in which these supplies are then used becomes less efficient, and there are numerous ways that could happen. Overall the system would suffer a loss in efficiency (and productivity), despite the local gain. And of course the reverse is also true – local losses in efficiency may be masked by overall gains in the system.

Second, and this is the most worrying, genuine local efficiencies can actually cause systemic inefficiencies in certain circumstances. As the Public Accounts Committee pointed out, there is a very big example of this in the NHS's efficiency drive. Nearly £1bn of savings are said by the Department of Health to have come from improving patient throughput in hospitals – getting them out of the door faster. But as the PAC points out, readmission rates have been steadily rising over the same period.

It is not unreasonable to link the two – more patients are having to return to hospital after being turfed out too early. No one has yet calculated the cost of this, but again it is not impossible that it could offset the efficiency gains entirely, not to mention the inconvenience and pain it might be causing patients.

The PAC concluded – rightly – that government departments were concentrating on a narrow set of efficiency projects and not looking at "efficiency in the round". Periodic bouts of efficiency scrutiny may be an inevitable necessity in public services, where the pressures of competition are weak or non-existent.

Even a cursory glance at large private sector organisations would show that even with market pressures to contend with, they too are often forced into such periodic efficiency binges.

But like all binges, however gratifying they might be in the short term you have to be aware of the bigger picture and the longer term consequences.

Chapter 44. Reviewing the situation

Public Finance 21-09-2007

After the fallout from Northern Rock, next month's Comprehensive Spending Review has suddenly become a lot more interesting. Colin Talbot charts the changes ahead for public spending and targets – and the challenges facing the new chancellor.

Events, dear boy, events. The famous words of Prime Minister Harold Macmillan, when asked what worried him most, must be echoing in the ears of new Chancellor Alistair Darling. As if the new New Labour government hadn't had enough of a baptism of fire – or rather of bombs, floods and foot and mouth – now it has a financial crisis.

In a few weeks (October 16 is pencilled in), Darling was due to announce what should have been a fairly unremarkable Comprehensive Spending Review and Pre-Budget Report (HM Treasury 2007) (the two being rolled up together this year because of the late appearance of the CSR) . The broad parameters of the review are already well known – a significant slowdown in spending increases and a small drop in public spending as a proportion of national wealth. Many departments settled their plans with the Treasury months ago and these were announced in last year's PBR and this year's Budget.

It even looked as if the CSR would be fairly uncontroversial as David Cameron's Conservatives decided to 'do a Gordon Brown' over the summer and commit themselves to sticking to the CSR spending plans if they came to power, in the same way that New Labour stuck to Tory spending plans in 1997/98.

The only real unknowns for CSR 2007 (HM Treasury 2007) then were the priorities the government would be setting for the next three years in the departments' Public Service Agreements and, of course, whatever rabbits Darling could find to pull out of his hat to make it look interesting.

All that appears to be a little more uncertain this week after the turmoil in the financial sector and, more importantly, its political fallout. The Conservatives' assault on 'public and private debt' after the Northern Rock debacle surely raises issues about their commitment to sticking to the CSR. They can hardly simultaneously hold the view that the spending plans are OK and that the government is running up too much public debt – unless of course they want to opt for tax increases to reduce the borrowing. More likely is that if they stick to their 'too much debt' line they have to start arguing for reductions in spending plans. Either way, the debate around the CSR looks set to be a bit more heated than anyone had expected.

Since its birth in 1998, the whole CSR process has been centred on the idea of 'money for delivery' – more money from the Treasury to spending ministries and public services in return for modernisation and, especially, improvements in services. More recently, efficiency has been added to the mix since the 2004 Gershon Report (Gershon 2004).

Delivery above all meant delivering against the centrally set PSAs. These were supposedly the pinnacle of targetry – central government holding its own departments to account for delivering and they in turn demanding better performance from the areas of public service they were responsible for.

Both the CSR and PSAs were hailed by their originators as radical innovations and seen internationally as part of a trend towards what has variously been called 'outcome-based governance' or 'budgeting for outcomes'. Before then, the UK central government had operated for more than 30 years with an annualised budgetary system known fondly as 'PES' – for Public Expenditure Survey.

The new system took a 'zero-based' approach to all spending programmes and the first CSR and PSAs covered spending for the three years from April 1, 1999, through to March 31, 2002.
Among the other significant changes were a split between capital and current spending and between 'annually managed expenditure' (AME) and 'departmental expenditure limits' (DELs). The former was fixed for only one year and covered volatile, non-discretionary areas of spending, such as benefits

and contributions to the European Union. The DELs were fixed, supposedly, for three years ahead.

Departments were also to be given much greater flexibilities between years, allowing them to bring spending forward or push it back, as long as they kept it within their three-year envelope.

This was all supposed to provide much greater stability in public finances, create opportunities for strategic management within departments, allow for long-term investment planning, and so on. Above all, it was meant to end the tyranny of so-called 'annualisation' – being able to plan only one year ahead.

The PSAs were meant to focus on the eventual outcomes of policy and hold departments to account for delivery of these outcomes. Outcomes in this context are the social or personal effect of government activities – having a hip operation is an 'output' or service, being able to walk again is an 'outcome'.

From the start, though, it was a little confusing about how the PSAs were supposed to work. They were talked about as 'quasi-contracts' but it was unclear whom the partners were. In one set of explanations, PSAs were an agreement between the Treasury and the 'spending departments', in another they were a contract between the government and 'the people and Parliament' about what New Labour would be delivering for all its extra public spending. Indeed, the government duly announced it would start producing an annual report setting out how it was doing against the PSAs and other targets.

Since 1998 (HM Treasury 1998), there have been Spending Reviews in 2000 (HM Treasury 2000), 2002 (HM Treasury 2002) and 2004 (HM Treasury 2004), ie, every two years. Then there has been a three-year gap until the 2007 review (HM Treasury 2007), which is also only the second one described as 'Comprehensive'.

The two-year Spending Reviews might have occurred every two years but they were still three-year reviews. For example, the 2000 one set out spending plans for the three years from April 2001 to March 2004. As a result, year three of each Spending Review from 1998 to 2002 turned out to be meaningless as it was superseded by the next review. So the whole process became known – in a classic bit of 'Sir Humphrey' Whitehall-speak – as 'a three-year spending cycle reviewed every two years'. You could not make it up.

What caused these deviations from the original policy? The simple answer is politics. If the original three-year cycle had been adhered to, the next Comprehensive Spending Review would have appeared in the summer of 2001, but Labour planned to hold a general election in the spring of 2001. As the new CSR was due to announce important extra resources for public services – especially health and education, two key political battlegrounds –, having the announcement several months after the election would have been a bit fruitless. So CSR2001 became SR2000 (HM Treasury 2000) and so on.

The reasons for the three years between the last review and the 2007 one (HM Treasury 2007) might also be political – CSR2007 will be Gordon Brown's first assessment as prime minister rather than chancellor and will offer other political benefits. If PM Brown is not forced into an early election, then a new two-year SR in summer 2009 (with hopefully better public finances and more largesse to dispense by then) would be ideal for an autumn 2009 or spring 2010 election.
Far-fetched? Possibly, but no more implausible than the whole SR/CSR explanation.

The timing issues have not been the only problems. The new system has not introduced quite as much stability at the macro-level as desired – there have been periods of both substantial underspending and significant overspending, especially in health recently. And while longer-term budgets might be good for Whitehall departments, there is little evidence that this has 'trickled down' to frontline services, where budgets seem just as volatile as ever.

PSAs have had a similarly rocky history. Despite their initial aim, until recently they were more about outputs and processes than outcomes. Thankfully, this has now changed but this has created new problems. First, outcomes are difficult to measure and the NAO's 2005 report, Public Service Agreements: managing data quality, and a follow-up (Comptroller and

Auditor General 2005) found significant problems with the published data. Secondly, they are generally long term and even more difficult to attribute to government action.

What happens to the whole CSR/PSA system under the Brown premiership will be very interesting. The chances are it will not be dumped – the previous chancellor has too much invested in the system for that – but we might expect substantial modification.

The first and most important issue will probably be who does the CSR and PSAs. They have until now provided the Treasury and the chancellor with some very strong levers over the rest of Whitehall. It is doubtful that PM Brown will welcome these powers remaining in the Treasury, so some shift towards Number 10 and the Cabinet Office seems possible, if not likely. Secondly, we are unlikely to see much change to the structure of the spending system and a probable reversion to two-yearly reviews.

But there is going to be some substantial change to the PSAs themselves. The reduction will continue – down from the hundreds of targets in 1998 to around 30. In previous Spending Reviews there have been a few 'cross-cutting' PSAs but it is expected that most of the new slim line set will be cross-government.

This doesn't mean departmental targets will have gone away – each ministry will now have a set of 'Departmental Strategic Objectives', which will be partly based on PSAs, partly on fallout from the recent highly critical Departmental Capability Reviews.

And PSAs themselves will not be quite as simple as they appear. Underneath them will be a set of 'Delivery Agreements', which will supposedly involve all the key actors in the 'delivery chain' for each PSA and include targets for outputs.

How this whole new set of PSAs, DSOs and DAs will work in practice remains to be seen. It is likely there will be just as many data-collection systems for the new setup as there were under the old. So spinning this as a 'reduction in targets', as the government has been doing, is mildly misleading. It is certainly a major change in the shape of the system, but not at present a reduction.

In the recent past, Treasury officials were complaining – privately – that the old system gave them insufficient control over departments. They said that outcome-based PSA targets were too long term, too difficult to measure, too unrelated to resources and too easy to fudge because of external factors.

The new DSOs and DAs are supposed to be much harder-edged tools for holding spending ministries to account. Whether they have achieved this, we'll see in outline when the CSR is published. It will take a lot longer before we see if the Treasury really has got a better tool kit in practice.

SECTION 5. GOVERNANCE AND POLITICAL ECONOMY

This section contains a few articles where I took more of a 'big picture' approach to the role of government in society. These are mainly about the thorny issue of how big government should be and how the public realm should be governed.

My interest in this area has grown over recent years – after this collection of articles was written – and is the subject of some of my more recent writing.

Chapter 45. Fall and rise of the state

Public Finance 15-10-2004

The state is dead, long live the state. After decades spent rolling back Big Government, state building is suddenly back in fashion. Colin Talbot reports on the turn-around.

State building – studying it, doing it, debating it – is suddenly back in vogue. After decades when any mention of the subject was an instant conversation-stopper, students are queuing up for courses in public administration. Worldwide, expertise in running public sector organisations is in hot demand.

How did this transformation come about? From the mid-1970s onwards, the world seemed dominated by the politics of 'rolling back the frontiers of the state'. Big Government was a bad thing and for some any public sector activity was a bad idea.

In the developed world, radical governments from Washington and Westminster to Wellington set about dismantling Big Government. Industries were privatised, services slashed, market forces introduced into public services and bonfires of regulations regularly lit.

US Republican president Ronald Reagan and UK Conservative Prime Minister Margaret Thatcher symbolised this movement, while in New Zealand it was a Labour government that implemented arguably the strongest set of anti-state policies anywhere. By the mid-1990s, even Left-of-centre politicians such as US president Bill Clinton were declaring that 'the age of Big Government is over'.

In developing countries, the International Monetary Fund and World Bank imposed 'structural adjustment', which meant dismantling many state activities, cutting back on state spending, liberalising markets, privatising state-owned industries and generally reducing the scope of government.

Meanwhile, the fall of the Berlin Wall in 1989 and the collapse of Communism in the former Soviet Union and eastern Europe seemed to ratchet up the rolling-back of the state and the growth of democracy to new proportions. Nationalised industries were sold off by the lorry load and new democratic governments elected. The liberal market state seemed home and dry.

The triumphant march of this new model seemed to be captured in the Francis Fukuyama book, *The end of history and the last man*, published in 1993 (Fukuyama 1993), which quickly became a bestseller and an even bigger topic for pundits everywhere. The popular interpretation of Fukuyama's book was that humans had finally settled on a single model of society that looked rather like... well, the US.

The end point of history was, seemingly, the liberal democratic market state along the US model – a small state sector (about 30%–35% of GDP) with low tax and low regulation, strong democratic checks and balances limiting the role of government and very limited welfare provision.

However, since the mid-1990s, a new element seems to have entered the equation – state collapse. The wars in the Balkans, the genocide in Rwanda, the collapse of Afghanistan and Somalia and the rise of HIV and AIDS in Africa all suggested deep political and institutional disarray. 'Failed states' suddenly became dramatically more important when a terrorist network using one of them as a base launched the devastating attacks of September 11.

At first glance, Fukuyama's latest book – State building (Fukuyama 2004) – seems to be the opposite of his 1993 tome. In this new book, he argues strongly for the idea that the old 'Washington Consensus' – what all the developing world needed was a strong dose of markets and liberalisation – did not work. The collapse of some states, such as Afghanistan and Somalia, and the problems in others (the Mexican and Asian financial crises) showed that the state matters and 'state building' is now a Good Thing.

The real turning point in ideas was, however, long before September 11 and was symbolised by the World Bank's annual 'world development report' of 1997 (World Bank 1997), The state in a changing world. The essential message of this report – and Fukuyama's new book – is that state size and state capacity are not the same thing. While too much of one – size – may arguably be a bad thing, too little of the other – capacity – very definitely is a bad thing.

State collapse, the growth of HIV/AIDS in Africa, financial crises in developing countries, the growth of the shadow economy and international crime, such as people trafficking and drugs, can all be attributed to state incapacity – its inability to impose and sustain rules of conduct in society or provide basic services. So, goes the argument, state building – especially institution building – is OK.

The truth is that even in the developed world the whole rhetoric of 'rolling back the state' policies of the final quarter of the past century was only ever partially successful. State size, as measured by spending and employment, stabilised rather than rolled back. Overall, countries in the Organisation for Economic Co-operation and Development hardly changed at all. In supposedly strongly 'reforming' states such as the US and UK, the changes were very modest in overall terms. A few countries, including New Zealand and Ireland, did reduce state size, but others increased it.

The reforms probably did halt the seemingly inexorable rise in state size since the end of World War Two, but it did not roll back very much, if at all, in most advanced countries. As it has become increasingly clear that the public sector is here to stay, and is an important part of advanced countries' well-being, it has gradually become fashionable to think about how best to organise and manage public services.

In the developing and transitional countries, the impact was much more dramatic and, in most cases, detrimental. Privatisation, structural adjustment and liberalised markets certainly happened on a grand scale but they were often disastrous. As most sensible analysts now believe, these changes work only if state capacity is sufficient to provide a firm framework of regulation and basic services. The impact of 'failed states' serves only to emphasise this conclusion.

So, studying the state – how it is constructed, governed and legitimised – seems suddenly to be back in fashion. Fukuyama's book is only the tip of a surge of studies encompassing state building, social capital, governance, public services and a range of issues about what a state can do, should do and how it does it (including whether the individual state is still a viable model).

The 1980s and 1990s often seemed to be the decades of the Master of Business Administration – the internationally recognised symbol of training for running private business in competitive markets. MBA became a widely known term and a synonym for the new entrepreneurial spirit of the age. Everyone wanted one – even thousands of public servants queued up to get them. It was the badge of the new zeitgeist.

Today, a new set of initials probably captures the rehabilitation of government. A global wave (or at any rate ripple) in the creation of 'Masters of Public Administration' (MPAs) seems to be happening. The MPA has long been a standard in the US but was until recently largely confined to there. Today in Europe – east and west – dozens of MPA programmes have sprung up. China has launched more than 50 in the past five years, training thousands of postgraduates. The Australian and New Zealand governments and a group of 11 universities have come together to launch the ANZ School of Government, focused around a big MPA programme. In the UK, from only one or two courses a decade ago, provision is expected to reach about 20 this year and maybe double that within another couple of years.

The pendulum has clearly swung back to recognise that markets cannot solve everything and the state really does matter. One US writer made a rather telling point: as New York's Twin Towers blazed after the two aircraft crashed into them, public servants – fire fighters, police, paramedics – were making their way into the buildings while their private sector occupants were leaving. Even in the US, this has given a new life to understanding that 'state building' is maybe not such a bad thing after all.

Chapter 46. A Rock and a hard place

Public Finance 25-01-2008

This year has got off to a somewhat odd start, with the word that dared not speak its name – nationalisation – back from the dead, and even state ownership of body parts up for debate.

The N word is back. No, not the race one – but **nationalisation**.

The most obvious place it has reappeared is in the prolonged debate about what to do about Northern Rock. But it has cropped up in several other policy controversies as well – not least Prime Minister Gordon Brown's suggestion that we should nationalise corpses (which is effectively what the organ transplant proposals amount to).

In some ways, this is a quite weird resurgence of an old debate that many thought had been laid to rest in the 1990s. When the dust settled on the big Conservative privatisations of the 1980s and New Labour abandoned Clause Four (the section of the Labour Party constitution that committed it to widespread public ownership), it seemed we had reached a new national consensus about the role and scope of the state.

The old Left-Right debate about the state versus the market seemed almost irrelevant. There was talk of the new 'post-ideological age'. But old fault lines in politics never seem completely to go away.

There is, of course, a large dose of political theatre in the debate about Northern Rock. The Tories spotted an opportunity to hark back to the bad old days of Labour, when the Militant Tendency ran rampant and nationalised industries were almost a synonym for the 'British disease'. Just when we thought the French had taken on our old mantle, here we are back to debating public ownership, say the Cameroonies.

Most of the debate in the past decade has actually been the other way, ie, rows within the labour and trade union movement about the steady trickle of New Labour denationalisations. Most of these have been relatively easy for the government, reflecting the much-weakened position of the Labour Left and trade union activists. A few have proved rather embarrassing for other reasons – such as the appallingly badly handled Qinetiq sale. Here, it has been the auditors and Parliament that have caused the government pain rather than the Left.

The truth is, of course, that political rhetoric – from both Left and Right – has never even remotely matched reality. Throughout the twentieth century, first Liberal and later Conservative governments were involved in both nationalisations and expanding state provision across a range of areas. The Thatcher government – committed to 'rolling back the frontiers of the state' – presided over the highest level of public spending, as a proportion of national wealth, over the past 50 years, while Labour produced the lowest (in 1998). And Labour never got anywhere near nationalising the 'commanding heights' of the economy.

True, the 1980 privatisations saw the state withdraw from some obviously commercial areas like car production. Some of the withdrawals from more naturally monopolistic areas, such as power, railways and water, remain a bit more controversial and problematic. But, interestingly, public spending as a proportion of gross domestic product hardly changed at all as a direct result of these privatisations – the current level (around 42%) is also about the 40-year average.

No major political party in the UK now proposes any substantial change in the boundary between state and the private sector. Under Tory plans, public spending would probably shrink slightly as a proportion of national wealth, while under the Liberal Democrats it would probably grow slightly. New Labour has more or less stabilised it (although the recent spending round very slightly reduced it – by 0.8%).

Nor does anyone propose big nationalisations or big privatisations. So the furore over the N-word around Northern Rock is largely political froth. The Conservatives are making mischief. The situation is also being gleefully exploited by some reporters, whose memories are clearly longer than their sense of proportion.

The truth is that a bank whose faulty business model fell foul of world financial conditions was in danger of triggering a cascade of panic. The government stepped in to prevent this and is now stuck with effectively owning Northern Rock. As Lord Eatwell pointed out last week, if you define ownership by who holds the risk, we the public already own Northern Rock.

It now looks increasingly likely that the government is going to adopt a very 'Third Way' solution of having Northern Rock in some weird hybrid public-private status rather than risk being accused of nationalisation – privatising most of the profits while nationalising most of the risk.

The issue of organ transplants and ownership of dead people's organs is much more tricky. Some Tories are ideologically opposed to presumed consent, and so are some religious groups. What this illustrates is that the debates about the boundaries between public and private have not entirely gone away, but today they are mainly either purely pragmatic (Northern Rock) or deeply moral (organs), rather than ideological.

Chapter 47. Democratic ghost in the machine

Public Finance 13-07-2007

The new prime minister's plan to give Parliament greater powers sounds good on paper. But, just like his predecessors, he has made major machinery-of-government changes without involving either House.

New governments nearly always reorganise the 'Whitehall Village'. More in hope than expectation, when giving evidence to the Commons public administration select committee last December, I suggested what should happen when the change of prime minister took place.

Instead of Gordon Brown turning up in Parliament and saying: 'Here's one I prepared earlier', there should be some debate and discussion before ministries are reorganised, and Parliament might even be involved.

On June 15, the committee issued a detailed and thoughtful report on Machinery of government changes (Public Administration Select Committee 2007a). The facts they unearthed for the report are fascinating: since 1947 there have been 154 'Orders in Council' to reorganise significant chunks of Whitehall. On only 11 occasions has there been a debate in Parliament. The last one of those – about the abolition of the Civil Service Department – was more than 25 years ago.

Does it matter and who cares? It matters a great deal, for several reasons. First of all, every reorganisation costs money. No-one has a clue precisely how much, because these things are never priced. But we can be pretty sure we are talking millions of pounds, if not hundreds of millions, over the lifetime of a Parliament.

The Treasury insists as a near universal rule that departments have to bear the cost of reorganisations within their existing budgets. This almost certainly means that there is a knock-on effect on 'frontline services', as it is very unlikely that these costs can be absorbed easily in ever more tightly squeezed budgets.

It is, of course, not just the direct costs that matter. Every reorganisation means some disruption. When the committee asked former Cabinet secretary Lord Butler how long it takes for things to settle down after a reorganisation, he replied: 'Longer than you think.' He added rather ominously that: 'I have come to think, and I probably thought this when in government, that the frictional cost of making changes very often does exceed the benefit.'

The pace of frequent reorganisations also means that things hardly ever get to actually 'settle down'. Former housing minister Nick Raynsford told the committee that in his eight years in government his role had moved from Environment, Local Government and the Regions to Transport, Local Government and the Regions to Office of the Deputy Prime Minister and finally to Communities and Local Government. In his view, this had damaged both institutional memory and understanding of what policy his unit was supposed to be pursuing.

All of this might be all right if the purpose of the changes were sensible in the first place. When Professor Christopher Pollitt looked at this issue in the mid-1980s he concluded that only about half the changes were about policy – in other words making changes to better enable implementation (Pollitt 1984). Almost as many were actually about egos in Cabinet and deal-making between rival factions.

Even those focused on policy were often as much about being seen to be doing something as actually doing it. And the beauty of continuous reorganisation is that nothing remains static long enough for anyone to evaluate whether it worked or not.
All of this led the PASC to conclude that what was needed was a more formal process of parliamentary scrutiny before major machinery-of-government changes are made. At the moment,

Parliament is involved because Orders in Council have to be laid before it. But that procedure is largely meaningless.

The 'affirmative' procedure, which means both Houses of Parliament have to have a positive vote in favour, has been used only once in the past 60 years. The 'negative' procedure, under which someone has to 'Pray against' for an Order to be debated, has happened only a few times because the government has a simple way of getting around it. It doesn't usually lay the Order until well after the reorganisation has taken place. In recent cases, this has included the Order being laid almost three months after the creation of the DCLG. The one for the ODPM took an impressive six months.

This isn't just a New Labour problem – John Major only got around to laying an Order authorising the creation of the merged Department for Education and Employment in December 1995, after announcing it in July (it lasted five years before being broken up again).

So when PASC chair Tony Wright declared it was like a 'constitutional Christmas' when Gordon Brown made his announcement about greater powers for Parliament, he was getting a bit carried away. After all, Brown had already done just what the committee had asked him not to, and carried out a big reorganisation without any consultation.

And the new Governance of Britain green paper contains nothing that would prevent that happening again, and again and again in the future.

Chapter 48. A delicate constitution

Public Finance 27-07-2007

The green paper on governance could end up looking more like a whitewash, unless Parliament's powers of scrutiny are strengthened, argues Colin Talbot.

If the government's green paper on The governance of Britain (Secretary of State for Justice and Lord Chancellor 2007) is 'constitutional Christmas', as some have claimed, it is unclear whether Gordon Brown is playing Scrooge before or after the ghosts got at him.

It certainly looks like an attempt to lay the many ghosts of Christmas Past – the decision to go to war, cash for honours, the powers for special advisers, public appointments etc – to rest through a constitutional revamp. But, like all Brown announcements, this one will probably leave some of the constitutional Christmas partygoers with a feeling of unease, as it gradually dawns on them what happened the day before.

There are indeed many good and welcome things in the green paper. But there is also a whole pack of dogs that didn't bark, not to mention some that did rather quietly. For example, on voting and House of Lords reform, the green paper says nothing new and makes no firm commitments. Indeed, in short order, Justice Secretary Jack Straw was announcing that nothing much would happen on Lords reform in this Parliament (ie, before a general election).

But to start by being fair to the new government, has anyone noticed that we suddenly have green papers again? Many of us thought they were defunct, but the government says – on both the constitutional reforms and other matters – that it is open to debate before decisions are made. That is very welcome, if it turns out to be true.

There is a lot in the proposals about strengthening Parliament and its ability to hold the executive to account. Changes to the use of Crown prerogative powers, many of which are to be passed to Parliament or put on a statutory basis, are massively overdue.

Some changes are almost comical – for example, the prime minister's right to appoint bishops in the Church of England has always been a farce and getting rid of it is of little real import, except symbolically. The real issue is the establishment of the Church of England in the UK constitution, something the green paper avoids, even though there is a large body of opinion in favour of ending the anachronism altogether.

Other decisions over war and peace are clearly substantial but Parliament has always been able, if it stirs itself over a major issue, to override the executive. There have been plenty of examples of a ruling party's majority disappearing over a major issue when the government has gone too far even for its own supporters. Holding the executive to account over the big issues is not the problem, it is in the day-to-day exercise of routine power that the British Parliament is so weak in comparison with many other western democracies.

Let's take a simple example – budgets. In most western countries, the executive presents a budget to the legislature that is then pored over and voted on in at least some detail. Specific allocations and taxes might be thrown out or amended. In Britain, and solely by convention, Parliament has effectively given up the right to really scrutinise expenditure and taxation plans and instead just annually signs the cheques, as the Hansard Society pointed out in a report last year and the Treasury select committee has repeatedly suggested.

Such rights do not have to be enacted as in the US's dual-power relationship between Congress and presidency, which can lead to deadlock. But it also does not have to take the form of Parliament simply signing off the plans that the government presents to it either. There are many ways in which Parliament could be involved more actively, especially given the opportunity afforded by the annual cycle, which now involves a

Pre-Budget report in the autumn and a full Budget in the spring, and of course the two- to three-year cycle of Spending Reviews. On this, all the green paper offers is an opportunity to debate the plans and objectives of major government departments on the floor of the house. It is unclear whether this will be post-hoc, just reviewing past decisions, or timed so that Parliament can have some input into decisions before they happen.

When the Commons public administration select committee proposed, a couple of years ago, a debate in the house on Public Service Agreements before they were agreed, they got short shrift from the government, which argued that Parliament was there only for post-hoc scrutiny. Maybe the Brown government has changed this line, but if so it has not yet said so clearly.

The only real concession to Parliament's role in the expenditure process is to take up a proposal from the Treasury select committee to make consistent the way in which expenditure plans are reported. Currently there are three, inconsistent, systems – budget plans, estimates submitted to Parliament and finally resource accounts. It is almost impossible to match figures in these three sets of documents and understand any changes.

Whatever Parliament's role in these processes, there is a much bigger issue – does it have the capacity to carry out effective scrutiny? Our parliamentary select committees have very scarce resources.

Recently the House of Commons Scrutiny Unit has been established to help bolster this capacity and the National Audit Office has slowly expanded its role into supporting select committees other than the Public Accounts Committee. The recent case of the foreign affairs select committee asking the NAO to carry out a value-for-money audit of the British Council is a sign of this changing relationship.

But by international standards, the British Parliament has very weak capacity to analyse government plans and performance. The green paper says nothing about addressing this capacity issue, which would strengthen parliamentary scrutiny.

The green paper proposes that the government will at last put the civil service on a statutory basis. This commitment is included in the proposed Constitutional Reform Bill, which is part of the legislative programme announced by Brown. The suspicious might note, however, that the detail on the Bill merely says it 'could' include the civil service.

If the proposal is to simply enact in legislation what is currently established in various codes of conduct, we will see very little change. There are three crucial issues in civil service reform: accountability of the civil service to Parliament; scrutiny of senior appointments; and scrutiny of machinery of government changes. None of these is addressed in the green paper.

One of the headlines that greeted the green paper was that we are going to get US-style pre-appointment hearings for senior public servants. And, indeed, the Treasury Committee almost immediately announced the first such hearing – it has already interviewed and pronounced on Sir Michael Scholar, the proposed chair of the new Statistics Board.

Again there is more than a little spin here. In the US, Congress scrutinises and approves all senior appointments. Here, Parliament does not approve appointments and still will not do so under these proposals – except in the case of the chair of the Statistics Board.

In a very few cases, such as the civil service commissioner, the commissioner for public appointments and some inspectors and ombudsmen, Parliament will have a stronger say. In most others it will have a limited role, and even then be restricted to 'public bodies at arm's length from ministers'.

In other words, the most important appointments in the Whitehall village, the proposed mandarins, will avoid parliamentary scrutiny.

As reported recently in these pages, the incoming Brown government totally ignored the recent PASC report on machinery-of-government changes (Public Administration Select Committee 2007a) and the role of Parliament and seems set to continue doing so, as there is no mention in the green paper of them.

So what can we conclude from all this? Certainly, in terms of strengthening Parliament's ability to scrutinise and challenge the executive in the day-to-day running of the government, these proposals overall do little to change existing relationships. Nor are they likely to make the civil service component of the executive very much more accountable. There are some promises and hints of future possibilities, but little is offered concretely.

Indeed, it would be a modern parable of Scrooge-sized proportions if Gordon Brown PM were to start behaving very differently from the Chancellor Brown who spent ten years manipulating the Whitehall machinery to accumulate ever-greater powers in the Treasury. He had ample opportunity with his spending reviews and Public Service Agreements to really engage Parliament and failed to do so. Still, we can always live in hope.

FOREIGN AFFAIRS

This final section contains just a few articles I wrote in this period about events elsewhere – the USA, Japan and France – all places I have visited several times and have done some work with their governments.

Some relate closely to themes running through this collection whilst others are rather more detached – my thoughts straight after 9/11 about the nature of Islamic fundamentalist terrorism.

Chapter 49. Tough on Terrorism, Tough on the Causes of Terrorism

PA Times 21-09-2001

I spent the week of the awful events in New York and Washington in South Africa, with many colleagues from their public policy and administration community. It made me reflect on how two organisations that had both been called "terrorist" – the African National Congress (ANC) and the apartheid state – eventually reached a peaceful settlement. And it made me realise why no such compromise is possible with those who attacked the World Trade Centre and the Pentagon.

UK Prime Minister Tony Blair first used the tough slogan above in relation to crime some years ago. A balanced response from democratic people to the utterly appalling events in New York and Washington has to look closely at how we both make sure justice is obtained, by whatever means are necessary, and that we remove the fertile soil in which terrorism grows.

We must reflect on what exactly is the terrorist menace we are confronting. We need to distinguish here between two distinct types of terrorist activities and terrorist organisations. The (Irish Republican Army) IRA, the Basque Euskadi ta Askatasuna (ETA), the Irgun, Hezzbolah, Al Fatah, and even the ANC of South Africa, are or have been, terrorist organisations fighting for causes they believe to be just.

They believe or believed – rightly or wrongly – that their specific people – the Irish, the Basques, the Jews, the Lebanese, the Palestinians, or South Africa's majority – had a legitimate cause. They often received explicit or tacit support from a wide section of their populations. In every case they carried out specific actions which by any civilised standards are barbaric and which killed innocent civilians.

Historically it has often been the case that one set of terrorist activities – the protestant Ulster Volunteers in 1920s Ireland or the Zionist Irgun in 1940s Palestine – have led to settlements which simply beget another round of terrorism – the IRA or Palestinian groups today. So the first lesson we have to learn is we must find ways of producing just, equitable and lasting settlements to disputes over territory and rights.

Just because someone pursues a legitimate grievance with illegitimate means doesn't mean we can ignore the grievance. The only way to finally stop terrorism in these situations is to find a peaceful settlement, a compromise surely that recognises all people's rights. There are few examples of where a genuinely aggrieved people who have resorted to terrorism (however wrongly) have been stopped by force alone, except of a genocidally unacceptable kind. While security and law enforcement are vital, they will not solve the problem alone.

The peace process in Ireland, for all its faltering nature, and especially the democratic transition in South Africa have lessons for us all. South Africa's negotiated peace involved compromises on all sides, it involved a new tolerance for each other's rights and it involved purging old wounds through the Truth and Reconciliation Commission.

The leading democratic nations of the world have a duty to start seeking and enforcing such settlements much more even-handedly and not merely when it is convenient to geo-politics or garnering votes back home.

Having said all of that, the terrorist threat posed by attack on the Pentagon and World Trade Centre is of an entirely different order. Whilst the terrorist networks involved may gather their supporters from those disgruntled by more specific grievances, their organisations are waging an ideological war. They seek not to achieve a specific righting of wrongs – against the Palestinians for example – but to overthrow a whole system – e.g., secular liberal democracy.

These groups are just as ideological as the 1970s Red Army Faction in Europe or the Symbionese Liberation Front, or more recently the Militia movements which led to the Oklahoma City bombing in the US. They simply have a different set of ideas and a different vision of an alternative society that they seek to create through terror – that of an intolerant, autocratic theocracy.

Because these groups are so ideologically, almost hermetically, sealed against any outside pressures, they are willing to commit atrocities on a scale rarely contemplated by more limited groups. The IRA, for example, could almost certainly have hit a UK nuclear power station or carried out some similarly catastrophic attack over the past 30 years. They did not, not because of any inherently more civilised approach to terrorism but simply because such an attack would have seen their popular hinterland evaporate overnight and destroyed their political base.

The second lesson we have to learn is that whilst there can be compromise and settlement with specific groups with specific grievances (the IRA or ANC), there is no compromise possible with these ideologically based forces.

This leads immediately to a third conclusion – our strategy to defeat these ideologically based groups must encompass settling genuine grievances in order to remove their 'hinterland', isolate them and eventually crush them. If we fail to resolve the genuine grievances that create fertile soil for their activities, we will find it exceedingly difficult to defeat them. But we also have to realise that this is a war – however you define it – that has to be fought through to victory. These groups cannot be negotiated with – they simply have to be defeated. Their grievances have no legitimacy whatsoever and their aims are completely antithetical to the values of democracy. They would rip up the Universal Declaration of Human Rights – we must defend it.

Moreover, because they reject any basic democratic and legal values and operate far beyond the remit of normal justice systems, we may need to use extraordinary measures to defeat them. That of course includes military action – preferably as surgical as possible even if it means more risk to our own side.

Collateral damage may not concern many in the US and beyond too much at the moment, but it only helps to provide more recruits and support for the terror networks and is ultimately counter-productive (as well as being morally wrong). We need also to consider other means – for example, the hijackers in the US used money that had somewhere to have gone through the banking system. There is more than one way to cut off their supplies.

Hence we have to be tough on terrorism and tough on the causes of terrorism – never more so than after last week's unspeakable events.

Chapter 50. JAPAN – Whole lot of shaking up going on

Public Finance 21-07-2006

Japan's Government Policy Evaluation Act bears a passing resemblance to Whitehall's Public Service Agreements. But it is part of a deeper and more extensive reform to take the politics out of public works.

Japan's Prime Minister Junichiro Koizumi is perhaps best known in the West for his spectacular hairstyle, his love of Elvis and his radical attempts to reform the way Japan's government and public services work. His government is much less well known for one specific aspect of reform – the innocuous-sounding Government Policy Evaluation Act, passed in 2001.

In June, I travelled to Tokyo as a guest of Soumusho, the interior ministry, to speak at a conference reviewing the Act's progress four years on from its implementation in 2002.

The Act requires all government ministries and agencies to produce performance evaluations. And they do – to the tune of about 10,000 a year. This is, by any standards, a massive undertaking. It makes the 160 or so Public Service Agreement targets set for our central government ministries pale into insignificance. The Japanese do things in a very determined way.

The rhetoric surrounding the Act is very similar to that heard in many democratic capitals in recent years, as various forms of results reporting have been introduced – from the UK's PSAs to the United States' Government Performance and Results Act. Even the French, after seemingly considering all this 'performance' stuff to be some sort of Anglo-Saxon aberration, have now adopted a rather similar set of policies.

But as with many things Japanese, the surface appearance – omote – isn't always quite what is going on behind the scenes – ura. The Act is certainly a general attempt to introduce some sort of results reporting into Japanese public administration, but it also has a very specific target: Japan's public works programmes.

Public works in Japan have a unique role. From the middle of the 1950s, they played a crucial part in maintaining the stability of Japanese politics, helping to keep the Liberal Democratic Party in power for almost four decades. In the early 1990s, this role was exposed in a series of corruption scandals, but these were only a symptom. The underlying problem was that Japan's whole post-war political system was built, at least partly, on the systematic use of extensive public works to 'buy' votes and influence for the LDP, especially in the rural areas favoured by the electoral system.

Thus, the Act is focused on reforming a key element of the Japanese system – the nexus of the public works bureaucracy, construction companies and politicians who traditionally have used these projects to garner support. So, out of 10,000 evaluations a year, around three-quarters are focused on cutting public works, partly or completely – by more than half before the projects have even started.

This is a very different context from the introduction of PSAs here, the nearest equivalent policy. PSAs have been about delivery in an expanding public sector, especially the crucial areas of health, education and criminal justice.

And the differences are not just contextual. Japan, like most other democracies, does these things by law, just as the Americans and the French have passed performance legislation in recent years. Here, the whole system is based on executive whim and can be swept away tomorrow without so much as a nod in Parliament's direction.

The other obvious difference between the Japanese evaluations and PSAs is the volume of information. While our government claims that we have only about 160 PSA targets now, this is dubious. Anyone reading them immediately spots that most of them are multiple measurements wrapped up as a single statement, and therefore portrayed as one target.

However, even with this weird system, our executive produces nothing like 10,000 (although we do produce similar amounts of performance data across the whole public sector).

The Japanese version may well evolve into more of a results management system, but at the moment it has a much more specific target, one that could have long-term consequences for Japan's already turbulent political scene. If it does, Koizumi will have left a legacy of change that will be felt in Japanese politics and public management for years to come.

Chapter 51. FRANCE – Vive la nouvelle entente cordiale

Public Finance 15-02-2008

France is struggling, like us, to cut back its public sector and devote more resources to the front line. But she would be wise to learn from the British experience before adopting our policies wholesale.

A couple of weeks ago I was invited to present a paper at a round table discussion at the French ministry of finance in Paris. No, not on the fall-out from l'affaire Soc-Gen, but on the more prosaic subject of public service reform.

Arriving at the Bercy area of Paris illustrates all that is good and bad about French public administration. Until fairly recently this was a run-down former industrial area of Paris, equivalent to London's Docklands. The decision to move the ministry of finance there – against howls of protest from its staff – was a typical French grand projet.

The massive scale of the building – which felt to me like the whole of Whitehall rolled together into one huge edifice – is truly staggering. And moving the ministry to Bercy has clearly worked: the area has revived.

But why does the French state need a finance ministry the size of some small countries? This is the sort of question French president Nicholas Sarkozy and his team have been asking. And they have – perhaps surprisingly, given the state of Anglo-French relations in recent years – been looking across the Channel for answers.

The round table, chaired by the public services minister André Santini, had been organised by Demos, the UK think-tank, which is working with the French government on their public services reform agenda, itself something of a first.

The Sarkozy government is fascinated by UK reforms – both under Thatcher and Blair (and sometimes, perhaps understandably, it confuses the two).

Indeed, the French public services reform programme has some aspects of both. Sarkozy's over-arching aim is clearly 'rolling back the frontiers of the state' à la Thatcher, but mainly by reducing the size of public spending in relation to national wealth, and within that the proportion of spending on administration.

Thus, Sarkozy proposes to cut public service numbers by 100,000 over five years through a one-in-two freeze on posts created through retirements.

He intends to halve the number of ministries through mergers and reorganisations. These include, controversially, plans to merge the various branches of the armed forces into a single ministry (something we already have) and to merge the state intelligence agencies.

Less controversially, the government plans to amalgamate the unemployment and social security agencies along very similar lines to the creation of Jobcentre Plus from the merger of the benefits and employment agencies in the UK.

This has echoes of both Thatcher's and Gordon Brown's efficiency drives, as well as New Labour's 'joined-up government'.

More New Labourish still are plans for decentralisation and choice, and in some cases the proposals are even more radical than in Britain.

Thus identity cards and the issuing of driving licences are to be devolved to town halls, something I doubt Whitehall would countenance here. More services are to be provided online or through call centres, an echo of New Labour's 'transformational government' agenda.

And finally, in line with Gordon Brown's (supposedly) three-year spending reviews, France is to move to a three-year cycle.

The recent strikes and demonstrations by public service workers have been motivated mainly by two things – job cuts, but first and foremost the proposals to reform their pensions.

On the numbers, Sarkozy has already retreated somewhat – now one in two of the jobs not replaced in administration is to be reallocated to the services front line (sound familiar?).

Indeed, it would be ironic if the French government were to adopt the 'head-count' targets idea from the UK – the British government effectively dropped it again in last autumn's Comprehensive Spending Review (HM Treasury 2007).

The massive public sector strikes in France evoke memories for many of Labour's 'winter of discontent' or the protests against Thatcher, but the reality is far more complex.

Trade union membership in France is tiny – only 8% of the workforce, compared with 30% in the UK and even 12% in the US. And France loses fewer days to strikes relatively than Spain, Italy or even, again, the US. Compared with trade union strength in the UK in the early years of the Thatcher government, France's unions appear very weak indeed.

But they have broken the backs of reforming French governments before, mainly because of their stranglehold on essential services such as transport.

The French can learn from the UK experience of public sector reform – we've been at it longer – but they need to be aware of the problems and the costs of change as well as the advantages. We have a tendency to export only highly sanitised success stories. Faites attention!

Chapter 52. USA – Bush fire under control?

Public Finance 28-03-2008

Critics of George Bush have accused him of many things, from trampling on civil liberties to playing the dictator, but greatly reduced powers actually mean the presidency is more constrained than ever before.

Most of the coverage of the US elections has concentrated on who is going to win – there has been very little coverage of what they are going to win. What powers will the forty-fourth president inherit?

The conventional wisdom is that President George Bush and his supporters have tried to create an 'imperial' presidency, a term originally coined by Arthur Schlesinger to describe the Nixon White House.

According to this view, Bush has unbalanced the fundamental settlement in the US constitution, overriding congressional and judicial constraints, and is even accused of having 'stolen' the election from Al Gore in 2000. Bush is variously accused of trampling on civil liberties, assuming semi-dictatorial powers and centralising power in the White House.

A new book by Maxwell School scholar Al Roberts – The collapse of fortress Bush – systematically demolishes this view. Far from inheriting a new imperial presidency, John McCain, Barack Obama or Hillary Clinton will take over an enfeebled White House with worryingly little ability to steer the most powerful nation on the planet.

Roberts argues that many of the accusations levelled against the Bush presidency have been greatly exaggerated. Take civil liberties, which, notwithstanding Guantanamo and other infringements of rights, were subject to much greater curtailment under emergency powers during the Second World War, the McCarthy witch-hunts and the Vietnam War.

Roberts is not out to exonerate Bush, Dick Cheney, Donald Rumsfeld and the other neo-cons but to demonstrate that the presidency is weakened and growing more so.

Again and again, Congress, the courts and successful civil society actions have thwarted presidential moves to erode the rights of US citizens. To be sure, there have been some encroachments but they have been relatively small.

Roberts suggests there have been multiple constraints on the imperial ambitions of Bush and his cronies. The first is increasing institutional complexity. The executive side of the US government (the bit the president controls) is far more complex than it was 30 years ago. This makes it far more difficult to steer. Another element has been the controls introduced after the Nixon era, including a whole swathe of legislation, plus watchdog agencies and non-governmental organisations.

The context of government has also changed – markets have become more complex and powerful, with the recent lack of control that the president and the Federal Reserve had over the sub-prime mortgage crisis being an obvious case in point.
Information technology changes have made government more transparent, more leaky and subject to much greater instantaneous scrutiny. Pictures of soldiers dying in Vietnam usually emerged long after the event – in Iraq we have had 'real-time' reporting.

Ironically, the neo-liberal policies espoused by Bush and his Republican supporters have also undermined the presidency. By trying to limit federal spending, deregulating and systematically undermining the public domain, they have also undermined the powers of the executive. Cavalier deregulation of financial institutions and big business – from WorldCom and Enron to sub-prime mortgages and Bear Stearns – have led to numerous crises.

Finally, there has been a decline in trust and fidelity within government. Even presidential appointees have been less loyal to their patron than in previous times. In the wider military and civil services, both legitimate and illegitimate whistle-blowing has reached epic proportions. Roberts points out that 'Deep Throat' – Mark Felt – waited 30 years before admitting his role in exposing Watergate. Today, whistle-blowers are more likely to rush into print and cash in within months.

Roberts' book reminds us of a fundamental truth about modern democracies – governments and their opponents often have a vested interest in exaggerating the degree to which rhetoric has been transformed into reality. Instead, we should always be asking, what has really changed? And how does it compare to what has happened before?

Such realism is all too infrequent in much of what passes for political analysis these days. A President McCain or Obama, but perhaps less so a President Clinton, who's been there before, will find out just how true this is next January.

There are lessons here also for those who tend to exaggerate how far we have a 'presidential' style of government in the UK. Reality is almost always more complex. Government is not all-powerful. Ask Alistair Darling or Gordon Brown if they think they are in control of the financial crisis. If they were honest they'd say no, or at least, not a lot.

REFERENCES

Atkinson, A. B. (2004). Measurement of UK government output and productivity for the national accounts: Interim Report. Journal of The Statistical and Social Inquiry Society of Ireland. Dublin, Statistical and Social Inquiry Society of Ireland.

Atkinson, A. B. (2005). Atkinson Review: Final Report: Measurement of Government Output and Productivity for the National Accounts, Palgrave Macmillan.

Bichard, M. (2004). Bichard Inquiry-Report. London, The Stationery Office.

Bichard, M. (2005). Bichard Inquiry - Final Report. London, The Stationery Office.

Blitz, J. and N. Timmins (2006). Blow for Blair on spending review. Financial Times.

Bridges, E. E. B. (1950). Portrait of a profession: the Civil Service tradition, University Press.

Brunsson, N. (1989). The Organization of Hypocrisy - Talk, Decisions and Actions in Organisations. New York, John Wiley and Sons.

Capability Reviews Team (2006). Capability Reviews: The Findings of the First Four Reviews. London, Cabinet Office.

Carvel, J. (2007). Public sector targets to be scrapped. The Guardian.

Chancellor of the Exchequer (1998). Modern Public Services for Britain: Investing in Reform - Comprehensive Spending Review: New Public Spending Plans 1999-2002. London, Parliament.

Clarke, M. and J. Stewart (1985b). Local Government & the Public Service Orientation. London, Inlogov/LGTB.

Common, R., N. Flynn, et al. (1992). Managing Public Services - competition and decentralisation, Butterworth-Heinemann.

Comptroller and Auditor General (2005). Public Service Agreements: Managing Data Quality – Compendium Report (HC 476). London, National Audit Office.

Comptroller and Auditor General (2006). Progress in Improving Government Efficiency (HC 802-I). London, National Audit Office.

Curristine, T. and A. Matheson (2005). Modernising Government: The Way Forward, Organisation for Economic Co-operation and Development.

de Frisching, A., C. Blairs, et al. (1997). Prison Service Review. London, HM Prison Service.

Downs, G. and P. Larkey (1986). The Search for Government Efficiency: From Hubris to Helplessness. New York, Random House.

Eastwood, C. (1993). A Perfect World. USA, Warner Brothers: 138 min.

Frey, B. S. and A. Stutzer (2002). Happiness and Economics - how the economy and institutions affect human well-being. Princeton, NJ, Princeton University Press.

Fukuyama, F. (1993). The End of History and the Last Man. London, Penguin.

Fukuyama, F. (2004). State Building. London, Profile Books.

Fulton Committee (1968). Committee on the Civil Service - Report, HMSO, London.

Gershon, P. (2004). Releasing Resources for the Frontline: Independent Review of Public Sector Efficiency (Gershon Review). London, HM Treasury.

Hasseldine, J. (1998). <u>Using Persuasive Communications to Increase Tax Compliance: What Experimental Research Can (and Can Not) Tell Us</u>, University of Nottingham, School of Management and Finance.

Heclo, H. and A. Wildavsky (1981). <u>The Private Government of Public Money (2/e)</u>, Macmillan.

Hennessy, P. (1990). <u>Whitehall</u>. London, Fontana.

HM Treasury (1998). Comprehensive Spending Review - Aims and Objectives. London, HM Treasury.

HM Treasury (2000). 2000 Spending Review : Prudent for a Purpose, Building Opportunity and Security For All. London, HMSO.

HM Treasury (2002). 2002 Spending Review ´Opportunity and Security for All: New Public Spending Plans 2003 - 2006´. London, The Stationery Office.

HM Treasury (2003). 2003 Pre-Budget Report, The strength to take the long-term decisions for Britain: Seizing the opportunities of the global recovery. London.

HM Treasury (2004). 2004 Spending Review: Stability, Security and Opportunity for All: Investing for Britain´s long-term future

HM Treasury (2005). 2005 Pre-Budget Report 'Britain meeting the global challenge: Enterprise, fairness and responsibility'. London.

HM Treasury (2006a). 2006 Pre-Budget Report 'Investing in Britain's potential: Building our long-term future'. London.

HM Treasury (2006b). Budget 2006.

HM Treasury (2007). 2007 Pre-Budget Report and Comprehensive Spending Review 'Meeting the aspirations of the British people'.

HMSO (1994, 1995). The Civil Service: Continuity and Change. London, HMSO.

Home Affairs Select Committee (2005). Home Office Target Setting 2004 (HC 320). London, House of Commons.

Home Office (2004a). Bichard Inquiry Recommendations - Progress Report. London.

Home Office (2004b). SR 2004 PSA Targets.

Hood, C. (1998). The Art of The State - Culture, Rhetoric and Public Management. Oxford, Claredon Press.

Hutton, B. (2004). Report of the Inquiry Into the Circumstances Surrounding the Death of Dr David Kelly C.M.G. London, The Stationery Office.

James, D. (2005). The James Review of Taxpayer Value, The Conservative Party.

Jenkins, K., K. Caines, et al. (1988). Improving Management in Government: The Next Steps, HMSO, London.

Johnson, C. and C. Talbot (2007a). "Seasonal Variations in Public Management: disaggregation and reaggregation." Public Money & Management **27**(1).

Johnson, C. and C. Talbot (2007b). "The UK Parliament and Performance: Challenging or Challenged?" International Review of Administrative Sciences **73**(1).

Kelly, G. and S. Muers (2002). Creating Public Value - An analytical framework for public service reform. London, Cabinet Office Strategy Unit (www.strategy.gov.uk).

Lee, P. (2008). Public Service Productivity: Health Care, Office for National Statistics.

Lipsey, D. (2000). The Secret Treasury. London, Viking.

Lodge, G. and B. Rogers (2006). Whitehall's Black Box. London, Institute for Public Policy Research.

Lord Butler (2004). Review of Intelligence on Weapons of Mass Destruction: Report of a Committee of Privy Councillors. London The Stationery Office: 107.

Lyons, M. (2004). The Lyons Review: Independent Review of Public Sector Relocation, HM Treasury.

Macpherson, W. (1999). The Stephen Lawrence Inquiry. London, HMSO.

Marquand, D. (2004). The Decline of the Public. Cambridge, UK, Policy Press.

Moore, M. (1995). Creating Public Value. Cambridge, Mass., Harvard University Press.

National Audit Office (2007). The privatisation of QinetiQ, The Stationery Office.

OECD (2005). Modernising Government - The Way Forward. Paris, OECD.

Office for National Statistics (2001). 2001 Census.

Peters, T. and R. Waterman (1982). In Search of Excellence - Lessons From Americas Best Run Companies. New York, Harper and Row Publishing.

Phillis, B. (2004). An Independent Review of Government Communications, Cabinet Office.

Pollitt, C. (1984). Manipulating the Machine: Changing the Pattern of Ministerial Departments, 1960-83, G. Allen & Unwin.

Pollitt, C. and C. Talbot, Eds. (2004). Unbundled Government: A Critical Analysis of the Global Trend to Agencies, Quangos and Contractualisation. London, Routledge.

Pollitt, C., C. Talbot, et al. (2004). Agencies - How Government's Do Things Through Semi-Autonomous Organisations, Palgrave.

Prime Minister's Strategy Unit (2007). Building on progress: Public Services report. London, Cabinet Office.

Public Administration Select Committee (2003). On Target? Government by Measurement: the Government's Response to the Committee's Fifth Report HC 1264. London, House of Commons.

Public Administration Select Committee (2004). A Draft Civil Service Bill: Completing the Reform. London, House of Commons.

Public Administration Select Committee (2007a). Machinery of Government Changes. London: The Stationery Office.

Public Administration Select Committee (2007b). Skills for Government. London.

Raymond, K. (2006). It is too big for any one person to run. The Observer.

Roberts, J. (2004). The Modern Firm: Organizational Design for Performance and Growth, Oxford University Press, USA.

Schneider, F. and D. Enste (2003). The Shadow Economy. Cambridge, Cambridge University Press.

Secretary of State for Justice and Lord Chancellor (2007). The Governance of Britain.

Talbot, C. (1997). "UK Civil Service Personnel Reforms: Devolution, Decentralisation and Delusion." Public Policy and Administration **12**(4).

Talbot, C. (2004). "Executive Agencies: Have They Improved Management in Government?" Public Money & Management **24**(2): 104-112.

Talbot, C. and J. Caulfield, Eds. (2002). Hard Agencies in Soft States. Pontypridd, University of Glamorgan (for UK Department of International Development).

Talbot, C., C. Johnson, et al. (2004). Is Devolution Creating Diversity in Education and Health? Nottingham, Nottingham Policy Centre, University of Nottingham.

Thain, C. and M. Wright (1996). The Treasury and Whitehall - The Planning and Control of Public Expenditure, 1976-1993. Oxford, Clarendon Press.

Treasury Committee (2006). The 2006 Pre–Budget Report. London: The Stationery Office Limited.

UNICEF (2007). Child poverty in perspective: An overview of child well-being in rich countries. Innocenti Report Cards.

World Bank (1997). World Development Report 1997 - The State in a Changing World. Washington, World Bank.

Young Foundation (2006). Social Silicon Valleys, a Manifesto for Social Innovation. London, Basingstoke Press/The Young Foundation.

Printed in Great Britain
by Amazon